UKULELE
FOR BEGINNERS

Tips and Tricks to Play the Ukulele

ACADEMIC MUSIC STUDIO

© **Copyright 2020 by Academic Music Studio - All rights reserved.**

This document is geared towards providing exact and reliable information in regards to the topic and issue covered. The publication is sold with the idea that the publisher is not required to render accounting, officially permitted or otherwise qualified services. If advice is necessary, legal or professional, a practiced individual in the profession should be ordered.

From a Declaration of Principles which was accepted and approved equally by a Committee of the American Bar Association and a Committee of Publishers and Associations.

In no way is it legal to reproduce, duplicate, or transmit any part of this document in either electronic means or printed format. Recording of this publication is strictly prohibited, and any storage of this document is not allowed unless with written permission from the publisher. All rights reserved.

The information provided herein is stated to be truthful and consistent, in that any liability, in terms of inattention or otherwise, by any usage or abuse of any policies, processes, or directions contained within is the solitary and utter responsibility of the recipient reader. Under no circumstances will any legal responsibility or blame be held against the publisher for any reparation, damages, or monetary loss due to the information herein, either directly or indirectly.

Respective authors own all copyrights not held by the publisher.

The information herein is offered for informational purposes solely and is universal as so. The presentation of the information is without a contract or any type of guarantee assurance.

The trademarks that are used are without any consent, and the publication of the trademark is without permission or backing by the trademark owner. All trademarks and brands within this book are for clarifying purposes only and are owned by the owners themselves, not affiliated with this document.

Table of Contents

Introduction 1

Chapter One: What is a Ukulele? 3

    Ukulele's History and Origins 3

    Ukulele Described 5

    Conventional Misunderstandings About Ukuleles 9

    What Type of Music Can You Play on the Ukulele? 9

Chapter Two: Guide on Playing Ukulele 12

    Knowing Your Hands 12

    Holding the Ukulele the Correct Way 12

    Your First Chord (C6) and the Thumb Strum 14

    The C7 Chord and the Fretting Hand 15

    The F Chord 16

    Reading the Chord Diagrams 17

    The G7 Chord 18

    Practice 18

    The C Major Chord 19

    Rhythm Directs Music 19

Chapter Three: Understanding Ukulele Chords for Beginners 21

    Where to Put Your Fingers 21

    Explaining the Re-Entrant Method 22

    Understanding Symbols.. 22

    Learning to Play the Easiest Ukulele Chords 23

    Learning the D's, F's, and G's.. 24

    Learning about the B Chord... 25

    Learning the Very Important E Chord 26

    Learning the Other Minor Chords 27

    Learning the 7th Chords 28

Chapter Four: Top Tips for Playing the Ukulele........................... 30

    Get a Good Ukulele 30

    Hold the Ukulele the Correct Way 30

    Enjoy Yourself 31

    First, Learn the Basics 32

    Play, Take Breaks and Play Again 32

    Learn Music Theory 33

    Play Slowly 33

    Listen to Ukulele Players and Play Along................................ 34

    Record and Listen to Your Playing.. 34

    Finger Workout... 35

    One Final Tip 36

Chapter Five: Types of Ukuleles 37

    Types of Ukuleles... 38

    Concert Ukuleles.. 39

    Tenor Ukuleles.. 40

    Baritone Ukuleles 40

Specialty Ukuleles 41

Chapter Six: Notes of the Ukulele 43

Musical Scales 44

Notes on the Ukulele 45

Whole Steps and Half-Steps 46

Chapter Seven: Musical Keys and Chord Progressions 48

Chord Transitions and C Major Scale's Chords 49

Chord Transitions 50

Key of C I-IV-V Chord Transition 51

The Key of G I-IV-V Chord Transitions 52

Using V7 instead of V in Chord Transitions 53

Key of C Chords 53

Key of F Chords 54

Chapter Eight: UKE Fingerboard 55

Chapter Nine: Common Chords and Chord Substitutions 61

Chapter Ten: Lead Sheets, Sheet Music and Chords 65

Standard Musical Notation 65

Sheet Music 67

Chapter Eleven: Chord Vexation and Movable Chords 69

Physical Limitations 70

Uncommon Chords 72

Chapter Twelve: Chord Tricks 75
    Tonally Similar Chords 76
    Same Name, Different Notes 79
    Same Exact Chord, Alternate Fingering 80
    Same Exact Fingering with Different Names 83

Chapter Thirteen: Strumming 85
    Strumming Patterns 89
    Strumming from Sheet Music 93
    Strumming and Rhythm 93

Chapter Fourteen: Playing Melodies on the Ukulele 97
    Playing a Melody on the Ukulele 98
    Options to Play Melody 100
    Playing Durations on Tablature 102

Chapter Fifteen: Understanding the Anatomy of Sheet Music for the Ukulele 105
    Standard Music Notation within the Treble Clef 105
    Song Sheets: Chords and Words Only 106
    Tablature Showing Melodies and Chords 107

Chapter Sixteen: Songs to Play on the Ukulele 108

Conclusion 126

References 127

Introduction

Welcome everyone who is here to learn how to play the ukulele. Learning how to play this instrument can be a challenging task, but there is a lot at stake.

To encourage you, think about all those people around you for whom you would be a source of happiness and cheerfulness. The ukulele is a friendly instrument that attracts people to it, spreading happiness to all who hear it. But be cautious, the ukulele's liveliness is easily transmissible. Once you become an expert in its chords and songs, you may find yourself sharing it with your friends and building a rapport for yourself.

Rather than learning it for your friends and the amusement of those around you, you can also learn to play it for yourself. Go through this book, buy that ukulele you have always wanted and beat your way to success as a uke player.

This book mentions all you need to succeed as a ukulele player. There is plenty of info about the instrument as well, about helpful resources and about where to begin. We understand that you will start reading this book with zero prior knowledge of the ukulele and how it works, which is why we have designed this book to help you learn from scratch.

By the end of this book, you will not just be able to hold a ukulele, but will also be able to play it with proficiency. We dedicate our efforts to every melody you generate with the ukulele in your hand and to every smile you generate through the rhythmic music of this equipment.

Chapter One

What is a Ukulele?

The ukulele, a Hawaiian-originated musical instrument, is quite exclusive in its own nature. The ukulele has long played an important part in the Hawaiian culture. Nowadays, this instrument brings happiness, not only to Hawaiian people but also to thousands of people all around the world. Some of the questions most people ask about the ukulele are, what is the ukulele? How did Hawaiians get the idea to make this instrument? What are the different kinds of ukuleles? After going through the following paragraphs, you will have all the answers to the above questions and more. I know for some, history can be a little boring, but to fully understand the ukulele, let's start from the very beginning.

Ukulele's History and Origins

In 1878, there were a few places in the world where large quantities of sugar cane were produced, and Hawaii was one of them. After the opening of the new markets in California, farmers had to expand their work to satisfy growing demands. As a result, a large number of people from Portugal came to the island of Hawaii, increasing the Portuguese community on the island significantly.

Typically, when immigrants settle in a new place, they bring their own cultures with them. Since most of the Portuguese came from

Madeira, and people of Madeira loved their music, what they brought was a small musical instrument called the machete de Braga. It was a simple instrument consisting of four metal strings, but maybe its simplicity was why the locals fell in love with it. With time, the machete started to change; the immigrants who settled there implemented some of the qualities of other similar instruments that were famous in their country, and the result was the creation of the first direct ancestor of the ukulele we know and love today. It was made by three woodworkers who wanted to come up with something innovative.

It goes without saying that the ukulele instantly became popular. Nevertheless, we still don't know how it became a valuable part of the culture of Hawaii, and we don't know why the Portuguese so easily fell in love with the ukulele, although the answer is pretty simple.

An art enthusiast and the protector of the ethnic identity of Hawaii, King Kalakaua, when he heard about the ukulele, included it into the performances played at the royal gatherings. When the king gives something some importance, it automatically becomes popular for the local people.

After it became the national instrument of Hawaii, love for the ukulele reached the United States, and soon after that, the whole world.

Ukulele Described

Now we have a little information about how the ukulele came into being, let's discuss what makes it different from other instruments and how to play it.

Many people, who know a little about stringed instruments, typically guitars, have many incorrect ideas regarding ukulele. For most people, the ukulele is simply a miniature version of a guitar. And we cannot blame their way of thinking; they just don't have enough knowledge, so it is up to us to provide you with the relevant information.

A guitar and a ukulele have a lot in common - particularly the classical. We are discussing size, shape, and how the musical instrument behaves and works. A ukulele is not just small; it has an entirely distinct type of tuning, meaning it has differing playing methods and differing chords. It is doubtful that a person who is an expert at playing guitar can play the ukulele right from the beginning. They may have the ability, but for this instrument's music theory, they would have to start from the beginning.

In contrast to guitars, ukuleles have four strings, and the ideal tuning is G-C-E-A. Besides having two fewer strings than most guitars, it also has distinct keys on the four strings. This means you cannot move the chords and scales of a guitar to a ukulele.

The ukulele is not simply a miniature guitar which you can put in your suitcase and take with yourself whenever and wherever you want. Rather it is a whole different instrument with its own unique features. Taking this into account, the making of the ukulele takes a whole different sort of method. Our next topic is about the parts or structure of a ukulele.

Structure of a Ukulele

Like every other variety of guitar, a ukulele has three main parts - hardware, neck, and body.

Hardware

Hardware may be a complicated little word, but it is the most general term to use for what we are going to discuss. Saddles, bridge, nut, and tuners are the things that come under this term. These are the same components that you would see on an acoustic or a classical guitar. Bridges and tuning machines are the most important hardware features in terms of function.

Just like an acoustic guitar, if the tuning machines are good quality, you will have problems with the ukulele, and the same goes for the bridge. Compared to the strings of the guitar, the ukulele strings experience much less tension. If you want your instrument to remain in tune, you must have high-end tuners on it.

Ukulele shapes and sizes can really vary.

Neck

The ukulele's neck is quite short, 21 inches on average, although this can be greater, depending on the ukulele model. Unlike electric guitars, on which you can use any kind of string you like, a ukulele needs a special kind of strings, mainly because of its short length. The two significant things you should keep in mind while selecting the strings are the length of the string and the tuning for which a specific string is used for. At first, it would seem complicated, but as time would move on, choosing the right string would become only second nature to you.

Body

The average ukulele's body is similar to that of a classical guitar, which is an hourglass outline with a regular upper and lower bout. The material and quality of the body will establish the type of sound it will produce. Different ukuleles can have different features such as sizes, shapes, and the type of tonewood used in their creation. We will discuss the different types of ukuleles in the upcoming chapters.

What Are The Features Of A Good Ukulele?

People who are new to the world of ukuleles usually ask this question, and the answer is not easy to explain. For now, we are going to stick to the two features of a good ukulele - first are the materials used in its making, and the second is the expertise of the one who creates the ukulele.

The best tonewood should be used to get the required auditory features, and the luthier (the one who makes the instrument) should try to use the most reliable ones. The standard tonewoods for a ukulele are Mahogany, Maple, and many others, but one of the best would be that of the Koa. The traditional ukuleles were made using Koa, which is why it is considered the best tonewood. Koa is naturally found in Hawaii, and it has been examined many times for its features. You will get the best tonal properties if you can find a genuine Koa ukulele. However, even if the highest quality Koa tonewood were used, it would make no difference if the luthier is not skilled enough, and this brings us the second important feature.

Although ukuleles are made in many parts of the world, the best ones come from Hawaii. However, the best doesn't come cheap. The reason the Hawaiian ukuleles are the best is that the luthiers learned directly from their ancestors who made the very first ukulele, so, naturally, they would have more knowledge and expertise as compared to other luthiers around the world. No one knows about ukuleles better than the luthiers in Hawaii.

Compared to the acoustic guitar, the size of the ukulele might produce a lower volume and a higher tone, which leaves the luthier with less room for error. The first strum on a faulty ukulele would disclose all its secrets; it might not be obvious to someone who's a beginner, but an experienced player would instantly know that something is not right.

> **TIP: When buying a ukulele, try to find one that you can afford and is easy to play. You can always upgrade to a better instrument later.**

Conventional Misunderstandings About Ukuleles

The popularity of ukuleles over the past few years has given birth to many misconceptions, and some of these fallacies have spread fast. The most common delusion people have is that ukuleles are easy to play, which is not true. This claim usually comes from people who have only watched some of the videos of Israel Kamakawiwo'ole. Israel had his own style, and he hardly played complicated chords. A ukulele has its specific chords and music theory, so it would take time and effort to memorize all of them.

What Type of Music Can You Play on the Ukulele?

This is one question that is asked quite a lot. Sometimes ukulele players get fed up with playing those easy-going Hawaiian beach songs. And they start to wonder what else they can play on their ukulele. Forget playing heavy metal, that's just not going to happen, but you may be able to play some jazz and blues. If you are prepared to translate the notes, you will essentially lose yourself in blues for hours, as both fingerpicking and strumming are deemed an authentic playing style.

Just like many other stringed musical instruments, you can find an amplified version of a ukulele. This type of ukulele will allow you to delve into a whole different world of sounds. With this, you can add different effects and easily adjust the volume. Furthermore, adding a distortion pedal to the signal chain can give you results that you didn't even know existed. The whole purpose of telling you all this is that don't limit yourself to what other people tell you. Rather, discover on your own what your instrument can do.

As small as a ukulele is, it can still perform wonders beyond people's imagination.

Is the Ukulele Worth Learning?

That is something you should decide on your own, but if you really want to know if you would be interested in it, find someone who owns a ukulele, or head to any music store and give it a try.

First things first, you should keep in mind that ukulele is not easy to play; you have to work really hard to get good at it. But once you start playing it, you will quickly get addicted to it.

A ukulele is as sophisticated as other stringed instruments, and its small size makes it even easier to carry. This is one of the principal reasons for the rise of its popularity. As compared to a fair starter guitar, a starter ukulele would cost significantly less. And if you want to join the ukulele community, rest assured this community takes care of each other.

Chapter Two

Guide on Playing Ukulele

Knowing Your Hands

One thing to keep in mind is that both the hands have a lot of work to do. Most of the people, even left-handed ones, will use their right hand as the strumming or speaking hand and the left as the chording hand, which holds the strings down. However, for some of the left-handed people, it is difficult to express their tempo using the non-dominant hand. What they can do is either flip their instrument around and design their own chord shapes or restring their ukulele. It is easy to restring, and it can relive left-handed people from exhausting annoyance. Throughout the following text, we may mention the right hand instead of the strumming hand and the left in place of the chording. Moreover, if you are left-handed, you would probably have to flip all the chord diagrams, as all of them are drawn in a standard right-handed manner.

You will find it easier to make chords if your nails are properly cut. You can have long nails on your right hand, as these can sometimes act as picks.

Holding the Ukulele the Correct Way

In every school, a lot of time is given to teaching students how to hold the musical instrument the right way. Until they are ready, students are given cardboard boxes and a stick to perfect their holding technique. Although this is not always the case with a ukulele, you should still focus on starting your journey with a good base. If you are careful at the beginning, later on, you won't have to forget the bad habits, and it will save you from damaging your tendons.

Whether you are sitting or standing, the first thing you should do is keep the ukulele close to your body. Use your right forearm to procure the ukulele to your chest, although some people use a strap to keep the ukulele in the optimal position. Use your left hand to gently hold the ukulele at the place where the headstock meets the neck. When sitting, don't use a chair with arms. Until you are confident about your skills, sit near the edge of the seat. To make it easier, put your right leg over the left and let the ukulele slightly sit on your thigh. Throughout the whole process, remember to relax your shoulders and breathe often.

TIP: Don't hold the instrument too tightly. Have a loose, relaxed grip with as little tension in your body as possible.

Your First Chord (C6) and the Thumb Strum

With a slight arch to your left-hand fingers, place them between the frets; your thumb would be behind the neck, right beneath your index finger. From top to bottom, the strings are numbered as 4-3-2-1. Use your thumb to gently stroke each of the strings. The optimal place for strumming is right next to the place where the neck meets the body, but if you are comfortable strumming anywhere else, it is fine. While strumming, say the words of the classical song, "My Dog Has Fleas" related to the ukulele tuning, along with the pitches (G-C-E-A) and the numbering of the strings (4-3-2-1).

You hear a nice soothing sound, right? Now with a steady rhythm, strum all the strings from top to bottom; 1-2-3-4 and 1-2-3-4 and sing the song, Row your Boat. With time you will learn to use other fingers for strumming, but still, to build up your base, you should focus on those steady down stokes.

The chord you have been producing up until now with your thumb strum is known as C6. It is a chord produced when all the strings are left open, which is when you don't use your left-hand for chording, and it comprises of the G-C-E-A notes. As mentioned in the previous chapter, these notes are the ideal tuning for the strings of the ukulele, known as "C tuning." Sometimes old books tell you to tune your ukulele to lower Bb tuning, and in Canada, most people tune to D tuning, which is higher. The modern books and the music on the internet would ask for C tuning.

The C7 Chord and the Fretting Hand

Assume you have a hand puppet on your left hand, and you are trying to make it talk. You would find your fingers in line, trying to tap on your thumb, and most probably, your wrist would be straight. Now turn the face of the puppet towards yourself, bring it around, put the neck of the ukulele in its mouth, and find the first string from the bottom, which is the A string. With a slight curve to your fingers, place your finger-tips between the frets with your index, middle, ring, and pinkie finger on the first, second, third, and fourth frets, respectively. Your wrist should still be straight, and your thumb should likewise be right beneath the index finger behind the neck of the ukulele. Lift every other finger except the index finger, and it should be on the first string, first fret. Now, if the instrument weren't there, your hand would be making an "OK" sign with your index finger touching the thumb and a gentle arch to each of the fingers; your wrist would still be unbent. With everything in place, strum the ukulele. Congratulations on producing your first C7 chord. Now you can synchronize this chording with a song like "Old Joe Clark."

After a lot of practice, you will get accustomed to chord shapes. Nonetheless, you can always rely on the chord diagrams. The first horizontal line on the top, which is darker than others, corresponds to the nut, and the other horizontal lines are the frets of the ukulele.

From left to right, the vertical lines represent the four strings (4-3-2-1). If you were to place the ukulele right next to the chord diagram, you would see that they would conform to each other. The dots you would see on chord diagrams portray your fingers, and sometimes there are numbers on the strings of the chord diagram; they are there to guide you to put the right finger on the right string.

By Alan Levine from Strawberry, United States - Working on the F Chord, CC BY-SA 2.0,

https://commons.wikimedia.org/w/index.php?curid=31211347
Holding an F Chord

The F Chord

The fingers of the chording hand, index through pinky, are numbered as 1-2-3-4, respectively. In the following text, we may address the fingers by their names, just for the sake of simplicity. As mentioned before, when the C7 chord is played, your index finger is on the first string's first fret. Move that fingertip to the first fret of the second string, and put the middle finger's tip on the second fret, fourth string (the string at the top). What you just made is the F chord. Now strum this chord. Ensure that your fingers are not touching any other strings, and you are using just the tips of your index and middle finger, or else the chord would not sound right. When you are practicing, pay attention to how your wrist and thumb are. Prevent them from making any inappropriate forms and keep them relaxed. This is the time to build useful habits. While experimenting between the F and C7 chord, you will see that the middle finger leaves off the fourth string and the index finger moves down from the second string to the first, the fret doesn't change. Think about how the fingers move between one chord and the other. Once you get an idea of the flow, strum few slow beats on both the chords and foresee how the flow takes place. When you succeed in doing this, you will know either you have to lower the number of beats, or you have to increase the speed.

Reading the Chord Diagrams

Most of the time, common songs are written with the chord diagrams or the chord names above them; this is known as the "campfire style." In chord diagrams where the syllable changes, the chords are mentioned directly above these changes. Consider the song "Happy Birthday to You," which is the embodiment of a song everyone is familiar with. It is the song that you can easily play by using the first two chords you have learned so far.

The pitch to start is C. Before taking a start, sing the song to yourself and locate your note on the third string. The song has a rhythm of 1-2-3, 1-2-3. By holding a C7 chord, strum that rhythm and then sing "Happy"…on the third beat, then switch to F for "Birth" and so on. While strumming, singing, and changing chords, the target is to make a constant rhythm.

The G7 Chord
To learn the G7 chord set your fingers the same as always for F chord. Place the index finger on the second string. Move the middle finger on the 3rd string and place the fingertips of the ring finger on the 1st string, both the ring and the middle finger would be on the 2nd fret. To make this position possible, your fingertips and thumb should be properly set. The shape of this chord is that of a triangle pointing to the nut. Adjust your fingers until it gives a proper sound. It may take time to create the finger strength and positioning. What you just performed was the most difficult task in this lesson, so now give yourself some appreciation; you have earned it. You can switch to F chord in the same way as you have moved to C7 from F. Practice this shift and afterward try to move to C7 from the G7 chord.

Practice
Let's play a song because that will make practicing much more interesting. To sing and play the song "99 Bottles of Beer on the Wall," you need to play the chords in this order: F then G7 and then C7. I believe you will become an expert in the chord changes by the time you reach the last bottle. A traditional Hawaiian song, "Popoki Make a Cat," is another fun song you can play and sing using the chord changes mentioned above.

The C Major Chord

So far, you have learned about the C7 and C6 chords, so now you will learn about the C major chord. The same method of learning as C6 would be used for C major. Pretend to make a hand-puppet with your fretting or chording hand and bring that puppet around; put the ukulele's neck in the mouth of your puppet and place all of the four fingers on the first string between the frets, with the thumb on the back of the neck. Leave only the ring finger and the thumb on your ukulele; you will see that your ring finger is on the third fret. Now strum this chord; congratulations on making the C major chord. As the ukulele is tuned in C tuning, the C major chord is something you will be playing a lot.

> **TIP: You can also hold your hand like you're holding a tennis ball in it.**

You may have noticed that the sound of C major is different from the C7 and C6 chords. In the chord name, the "C" simply indicates its dependence on the note "C." The number or word after "C" shows the musical adjective, the quality or flavor they possess. We just say C instead of C major; because the major chords are used regularly, they possess a neutral "flavor" and are written without any adjective.

Rhythm Directs Music

Bob Marley's "Three Little Birds" is an eternal choice. It is easy to play and sing, and you may already know its tune and memorable lyrics. By using a strong beat, you can make this song more interesting, and it is a good chance to try some contrasting strum.

The rhythm 1 and 2 and 3 and 4 and 1 and 2 and 3 and 4, etc., is the base of the most songs we are familiar with. These numbers are the beats or downstrokes and are placed in groups of four; we call it "common time" because this rhythm is so common in music. In the song, the "ands" are the upstrokes. For the upstrokes, we use the fingers of the right hand, as it is difficult to strum with the thumb.

Now, imagine that you are over the kitchen sink and trying to shake the water off your hands; you would see it's a certain movement from the elbow, a small twist of the wrist, and flip of fingers. This is what a good strum should look like. It is up to you whether you use index finger or group of fingers, but the major thing is to stay calm and steady.

Now let us give a variety to our play. Play only the even beats: that is 2 and 4 for a simple backbeat strum. You can get another backbeat by playing only the upstrokes.

A very small, complex strum is the "doo wack-a do." By brushing the fourth string, you get a light, partial down strum on beats 1 and 3, but for the even beats, you give an intensified down strum, and later on, play the upbeat.

Chapter Three

Understanding Ukulele Chords for Beginners

Before we start learning the different chords, ensure that you have a good quality of the ukulele. When playing on a cheap ukulele, the required sound won't be produced, so you might think that you are the one at fault. I know that, for a beginner, a cheaper ukulele is more feasible, but saving some money on your starting ukulele means you are compromising on the quality. If you buy a cheap ukulele, you might not be able to generate the right notes, and it may keep on going out of tune, so you would have to re-tune it again, resulting in a lot of wasted time. The other thing you should be certain of is that your ukulele is properly tuned, else the chords and notes you will produce would sound awful.

Now let us start our lesson. The first thing you should memorize is which finger represents which number. From index to pinky, the fingers are numbered as 1-2-3-4.

Where to Put Your Fingers
The four strings of the ukulele are represented by the four vertical lines on a chord chart. If you have previously played the guitar, you would see the similarities between the ukulele tab and a guitar tab.

The first string from the left is typically the G string, and it can be the thickest string; however, this is not always the case.

You can tune your ukulele in several ways, and one such manner is the re-entrant method. The order of the strings can be different according to the type of tuning you are using. As most of the ukuleles are tuned in the re-entrant method, the G string is not the thickest; this is the C string. Keep in mind that all the charts are ordered as G-C-E-A (standard tuning of the ukulele), and when we compare this to the numbering of strings 4-3-2-1, it tells us that the 4th string is G, the 3rd is C, 2nd is E and the 1st is A.

Explaining the Re-Entrant Method

The re-entrant method is as popular as the standard tuning method. Soprano, tenor, and concert ukuleles are commonly tuned in the standard method. As a matter of fact, the baritone and tenor ukuleles are the only ones that are not tuned in the re-entrant method. The re-entrant tuning stops the strings from going to high from low. For example, the re-entrant tuning method is used to tune the Soprano Ukuleles. It is easy to get used to the size of the soprano uke, and that is why it is well-known among beginners. If you, as a beginner, were to learn on a soprano, you will easily be able to learn new chords on it.

Understanding Symbols

You just have to remember two important ukulele symbols on chord charts. One is the black circle, which is the most used one.

When this symbol is present, it means you have to fret a note. Where this symbol is present, a number would also be written to help you put the right finger at the right string. The other symbol is the white circle, which represents an open string. The G-C-E-A are the notes mentioned on the open strings. If you can remember these, it would help you a lot in placing your fingers at the right strings.

If you are a complete beginner, you might want to learn the symbols for the ukulele chords as well. A small m refers to a minor chord, and a capital M refers to a major chord. For example, if "Am" is written, it means "A" minor chord; similarly, if "AM" is written, it means "A" major chord.

Learning to Play the Easiest Ukulele Chords
You can learn the ukulele chords in whatever order you like, but learning them in alphabetical order might be the best way. Most of the books will first teach you the chords related to the C key, and later on the other keys.

In the previous chapter, we learned about some of the chords, specifically the C major, C7, F major, and G7. So we won't go through them again. If you need to look at them, just go to the previous chapter.

First, we will learn the easiest chords, and afterward, we will learn the harder ones. Let's start learning about the C minor, A minor, A major, and A7. After learning to play these easy C chords, you might think the ukulele is not that hard, but don't be fooled; these chords are just the tip of the iceberg.

With all that said, let's start. To make a C minor chord, you can either use a barre chord (using a single finger to hold different strings) on the second (C), third (E), and fourth (A) strings or use your three fingers; the fret is still the third one. The C minor Chord has other variants as well, which you can learn in the future. If you are a novice, we recommend that you should use your fingers instead of a barre chord.

For the A major chord, put the middle finger on the G string (4th string) of the second fret and the index finger on the C string (3rd string) of the first fret. A minor is just like A major or simply, A chord. To produce "A" minor, just place your middle finger on the G string's second fret. There you have it an A minor chord. To produce an A7 chord, put the index finger (first finger) on the C string's first fret. The C and A chords are already pretty easy to play, but if you have any experience with other stringed instruments, these chords will be even easier.

Learning the D's, F's, and G's

We will learn the B's and E's later; for now, we are going to learn another easy set of chords - D, F, and G.

The Fm (F minor) is a complicated chord. For this chord, you would have to place the index finger and the middle finger on the string G and E respectively; the fret for both of them is the first one. After this with your ring finger hit the A string on the third fret.

For the D chord, place the index finger on the G string, the middle finger on the C string, and the ring finger on the E string; the fret is the same for all of them, the second fret. The Dm and the F chord are very similar. To produce a Dm chord, just add your ring finger to the second fret of the C string, that is if you are already in the position of an F chord.

For the G chord, you will have to place your first three fingers very close to each other. You might feel a small amount of cramp, but with some practice, your muscles will get accustomed to it. To produce the G chord, place the index finger on the C string's second fret, the middle finger would go on the same fret but of the A string. The ring finger would go on the third fret of the E string.

Learning about the B Chord

The B major chord is something you won't play often, and that is good because it is tricky compared to the other chords. Though it is still important to learn, and you should save it for the time when you need it.

To play this chord, you will need to use a barre chord. Barre chord means to use a single finger to hold down multiple strings at the same fret. Usually, a barre chord is created by placing the first or the index finger on several of the strings at the same time. Still, compared to B chord, there are other complicated chords which demand that you use different fingers for a barre chord.

To create a B chord, use your index finger to fret the strings E and A at the second fret. Set your middle (second) finger on the third fret of the C string and the ring finger on the G string's fourth fret. This chord might seem a little difficult, so first, you should practice the other chords and try this chord some other day.

Since the Bb (B flat) chord appears more often in folk songs, it is more significant than the B chord. For a Bb chord, you will have to use a barre chord. Place the index finger on the E and A strings of the first fret. You would have to lower your wrist to be able to lay your middle (second) finger on the second fret of the 'C' or the second string and the ring (third) finger on the G string's third fret.

As this chord is often used in the key of F for the ukulele songs, you would be using it quite often. So you would have to practice a little harder to get good at this chord. If this chord is still a little difficult for you, then you should first learn the Gm7 chord. The Bb chord and the Gm7 chord are almost the same. In a Gm7 chord, everything is the same as the Bb (B flat) chord, except that you lift off your ring finger. Where necessary, you can use the Gm7 chord in place of the Bb chord, but still, you should master the Bb chord.

Learning the Very Important E Chord

It would help you plenty to produce the E chord if you put an effort in increasing the resilience and range of your fingers. You can accomplish this by doing some finger exercises daily. These exercises will also increase your endurance.

To create an E chord, begin with your index finger on the G (4th) string on the first fret. Then put the middle (second) finger on A string's second fret. For the ring finger, reach out to the fourth fret of the C string. There are other methods to play the E chord, but this one is the easiest.

In songbooks, you might find a different version of the E chord. This version would require you to use a barre chord on the fourth fret of the G, C, and E strings. Your index finger would go on the A chord's second fret.

As mentioned before, there are other versions of the E chord, and if you want to play the ukulele, you should at least master one of them.

Learning the Other Minor Chords

You are already familiar with some of the minor chords, but there are also other important ones that you should learn. The major chords produce a strong, happy sound, while minor chords produce a softer sound. Both the minor and major chords are of equal importance, so you should learn them. Let's check out the B, E, and G minor chords.

The Bm is a tough one. For this, use a barre chord on the second fret of the C, E, and A strings and also place the ring finger on the G string's fourth fret.

If by now, you have mastered the Bm chord, then there is nothing to be afraid of. To create Em set your index finger on the A string's first fret, the middle finger on the E string's third fret, and the ring finger on the C strings' fourth fret.

For the Gm chord, start with the index finger on the A sting's first fret. Then place the middle finger on C string's second fret. Lastly, your ring finger would go on the third fret of the E string.

Learning the 7th Chords

The 7th chords appear in jazz and blues songs very frequently, and they add a soul and a happy vibe to the music. As you are already familiar with A7 and C7, you know these are quite easy.

Compared to A7 or C7, the B7 is tougher. To create it, place a barre chord of the index finger on the second fret of G, C, and A strings. Your middle finger would go on C string's third fret.

For the D7 again, use your index finger to place a barre chord on the second fret of G, C, and E strings. Afterward, place the middle finger on A string's third fret.

The F7 is similar to the F chord. To the F chord, just add your ring finger on the C string's third fret.

To make the E7 chord set the index finger on G string's first fret. The middle and the ring finger would go on the E and A string, respectively; both the fingers would be on the second fret.

TIP: Take your time when learning the chords and don't skip ahead. Otherwise, you'll get discouraged quickly.

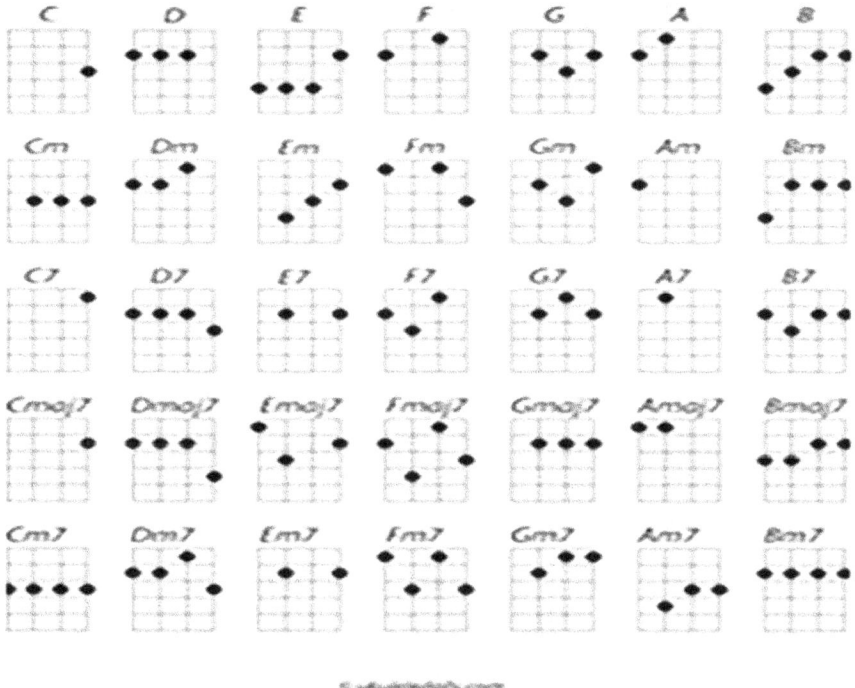

Ukulele Basic Chord Chart

Chapter Four

Top Tips for Playing the Ukulele

On the internet, you will find many of these top 10 tips. To those, I will be adding something from my personal tips for the beginner players. I will try my best to give you some useful tips, which will help you in advancing your journey into the ukulele world.

Get a Good Ukulele

If you are serious about playing the ukulele, this is the most important thing to keep in mind. One thing is certain; under $50, you won't find any good quality of ukulele. The major problem with the cheaper ukulele is that they don't stay in tune for long. I know this because once I made the same rookie mistake. For $45, I bought a Harley Benton soprano. The moment I would strum it, the E string would go out of tune immediately. I have shared my expertise with you, so now be cautious when you are buying a ukulele. To at least meet the benchmark, you would have to spend around $100. Anything lower, and the quality won't be there.

Hold the Ukulele the Correct Way

Holding the ukulele the right way will help you a lot in the years to come. As we mentioned in one of the previous chapters, if you are careful at the start, you won't have to unlearn bad habits, and it will save you from damaging your tendons. Whether you are sitting or standing, try different positions for some time. When sitting, don't use a chair with arms. If you are a beginner and you are not confident about your skills, you should sit near the edge of the seat. With your right leg crossed over the left, you can allow the body of the ukulele to sit on your thigh slightly, and you can let your strumming arm rest on top of the ukulele's bout. This would make the neck of the ukulele hover in the air. Either you are standing or sitting hold the ukulele close to your chest, and by using your right or the strumming forearm, you can procure it there. Some people use a strap to keep the ukulele in the optimal position, but I think it just adds unnecessary weight to it. At the start, you would have to practice harder, but afterward, you will get the results of all your hard work. Take me as an example; at first, I also had some difficulties, but now I play the ukulele while walking around the house. A bit of small advice: don't push the ukulele too hard against the chest; a ukulele is an acoustic instrument, so it needs room for the vibrations to spread through its body.

Enjoy Yourself

The ukulele is a fun and friendly instrument. Because of its small size, some people call it a toy, but whatever, when you play with toys, you have fun. Don't be fooled by its size; it is a completely unique instrument, with its unique chords and song theory, which can help you perform amazing things. To get good at it, you would have to practice really hard, so don't take it lightly. When you are familiar with even the very basic chords of the ukulele, you can still perform wonders with it. So play it to enjoy it, and without even knowing, you would be getting good at it each day.

First, Learn the Basics

When you go on YouTube or the different websites on the internet, you will find that you can perform wonderful things with the ukulele. Just like every other thing in life, for the ukulele first, you would have to learn the basics. Begin by learning the minors, majors, and other basic chords we mentioned in the previous chapters. Once you get good at the chords, you will be playing a lot of songs. Then you won't be thinking how to play a specific chord because by then, they will become second nature to you.

Play, Take Breaks and Play Again

Whatever you try to learn, there is a process of art and science behind it. Building up your "Muscle Memory" is the process I am referring to. It is the way by which your movements and motor activity are stored in your memory. For example, the chord progressions you would be playing would start to embed in your memory. If you are playing a chord transition from an E minor to the C chord and then to a B repeatedly, this progression would become so deep-rooted in your muscle memory that you would start to play it even without consciously thinking about all the transitions. So without focusing on how a song is played, it just becomes automatic for you.

To play a song without any difficulty, you would have to develop muscle memory, and for this to become possible, you would often have to take breaks. While learning different chords and repeatedly playing a song, take breaks often to allow your muscle memory to take in whatever you practiced. Whenever you go back to playing a song, you would find it easier, and it would become more automatic for you to play that song.

Learn Music Theory

It would be helpful to learn about music theory if you want to get serious about your ukulele playing. The language of the music is what is known as the music theory. You would become a lot better musician if you had some basic knowledge about music theory. If you can learn the essentials of the music, you would be able to do more experiments with your ukulele playing. And if you want to make your own songs, then learning the music theory is something you should make time for.

Play Slowly

When you have learned the fundamental strumming and some basic chords, in due course, you will begin to transition between chords. At first, try your best not to make any mistakes by playing as slowly as you can and practice this a lot with many different types of chords. Instead of being swift, remember the most important point is to be precise and accurate. When you start to play using tablatures, you should still try to play slowly. At first, don't try any difficult songs with many different chord transitions; instead, choose some easy songs with easy chords and remember to play slow. After you become good at those easy songs, try some of the difficult songs, and then you can start to work on your speed.

> **TIP: Learn to play with a light touch. The goal isn't to produce a loud sound. The goal is to produce pretty music.**

Listen to Ukulele Players and Play Along

If you are a part of a band, take your ukulele and play it along with your friends. If you are not in any band, no problem share the ukulele with your friends influence them so they can also play it. Even this doesn't work, don't fret, just go online on your phone or your PC and watch ukulele videos and play along with them. All of these methods will assist you in feeling the immense pleasure ukuleles provide. I know some people who just watched videos and played along with them to actually become really good at playing the ukulele. So carefully watch and listen to the rhythm, and gradually, you will begin to improve at playing the ukulele.

Record and Listen to Your Playing

It is intricate to play and also listen to yourself simultaneously. The recording is a way that can allow you to listen to your faults, and most of the time, just knowing about your problem can help you to correct it. Recording yourself can also help you to get accustomed to playing in front of a mic, so when the time comes when you decide to record yourself appropriately, you won't get the jitters.

Finger Workout

I know this might appear like a lot of work. You are already learning different chord shapes, different ways to strum, and how to transition between different chords; you would also have to do this finger workout too. This would help build up calluses (an area of the skin which has become harder due to continuous friction) on your fingers. It might seem odd to build up calluses on your fingers, but once you start playing the ukulele, it will help you to avoid getting your fingers hurt by the strings. The nylon strings don't hurt that much, but the steel-strings definitely do. I find the below-mentioned exercises to be really helpful.

First with your index finger on the first fret just behind the first string, pluck the string open, then with the middle finger which would be on the same string's second fret, then with the ring finger on the first string's third fret and finally with your pinky on the first string's fourth fret, pluck the string open. Now repeat the pattern moving upward with the pinky on the first string's fourth fret pluck the string open, then with the ring finger on the same string's third fret, then with the middle finger again on the same string's second fret and the index finger on the first string's first fret. Do this for the second string, then for the third one, and lastly for the fourth string. You should do this exercise a few times just before starting your practice. It will help you warm up your fingers and would also help in hardening your fingertips. You can also do this exercise with your right hand; it will help you limber it up. The other thing that helps in hardening the fingertips at the starting point is playing multiple times for less amount of time (for about 10 to 15 minutes) instead of playing it once for a longer duration, 60 to 90 minutes.

To harden your fingertips, you would at least have to play for 10 to 15 minutes, even if you have less time still do the finger workout. It will save your fingers from harm in the future.

One Final Tip

The fingernails on the fretting hand should be cut very short because your fingernails help produce the sounds your Ukulele makes. To make a clean fretting that would produce distinct sounds, the nails should be kept short and clean. You can let the nails on the strumming hand grow as these sometimes can act as picks, which can help produce great sounds.

> **TIP: Practice for a few minutes every day. Even 5 minutes a day can make a difference!**

Chapter Five

Types of Ukuleles

Ukuleles are so compelling and provide pleasure while playing. They provide freshness and relaxation to the mind. Its light and soothing tones make the chords sound so marvelous, and if we compare it with other instruments, then it is not so difficult to learn it.

Its four strings make it easy to play, and luckily for most of your favorite songs, it just requires the use of few chords. So buying the ukulele is the best choice among the musical instruments. Now let us discuss some of the types of ukulele.

AN OVERVIEW OF THE SCALE LEN

I have tried to get all of the pictures to the same scale, (1mn

Mini (aka Sopranino, Baby, Ukette, Piccolo, Sopranisimo, Micro, Midget, Pocket and a few other size related names)
scale length less than 305mm (12in)

Soprano (aka Standard)

**Scale Length
305mm (12in) to 355mm (14in)**

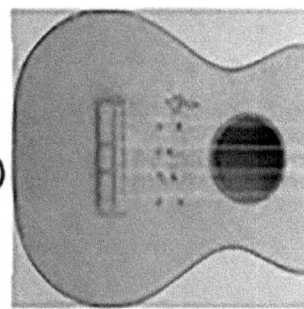

Concert (aka Alto)

**Scale Length
356mm (14in) to
405mm (16in)**

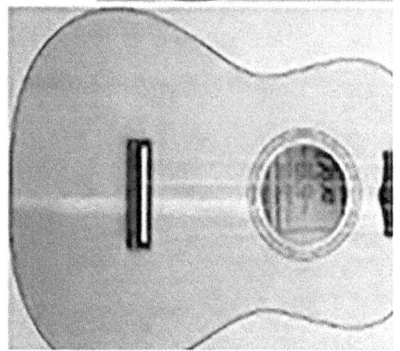

Creative Commons

Types of Ukuleles

Soprano Ukuleles

The soprano ukulele, for example, the Kala KA-15S, is the most favored and well known of all kinds of ukuleles. The sound of this ukulele is highly related to the original one, and in Hawaii, it is considered as the "standard" because its size is greatly compared with the real one.

This ukulele is smallest of all, and it consists of 12-15 frets, and these frets are narrower, which makes them easy to play, and the most important thing is that these frets do not demand the stretching of your fingers as much.

The soprano is the best choice if you want to play the most conventional ukulele. As the soprano is of smaller size, so it is cheaper as well, as compared to the larger styles ukuleles.

Specifications

- Its scale length is 13 inches.
- Its overall length is 21 inches.
- Its common tuning is G-C-E-A (HIGH G).

Concert Ukuleles

The concert ukuleles, like the Cordoba 15 CM, are next in size to the soprano. It also possesses the traditional sounding tone, but its sound is extensively fuller and louder. As its size is larger than the soprano so its frets are also wider, and this ukulele is the best choice for the one with bigger hands as for them, it is easy to navigate. Concert ukuleles have multifaceted sound.

Specifications

- Its scale length is 15 inches.
- Its overall length is 23 inches.
- Its common tuning is G-C-E-A (High G).

Tenor Ukuleles

Substantial to both soprano and concert ukuleles are the tenor ukuleles, like the Luna Tattoo Mahogany. They offer even more extensive sound. Because of their amazing sound, they are famous for professional musicians. In soprano and concert ukulele, we use only the high G, but as for tenor, we can fit it with lower G string as well as with high G string.

When you want a moving fretboard and deeper tone in your ukulele, then a tenor ukulele is the best. Otherwise for classical sound, the soprano and concert are better.

Specifications

- Its scale length is 17 inches.
- Its overall size is 30 inches.
- Its common tuning is D-G-B-E.

Baritone Ukuleles

The baritone ukulele is related to the standard guitar size, for example, the Kala KA-B. Like the highest four strings on a guitar, it is tuned in the same way. Baritone ukulele does possess the pure ukulele's feeling and sound, but their sound is not as light as that of soprano and concert ukuleles, nor they create so much resonance.

For the beginners, the baritone ukulele is possibly not for them because its tuning and shapes of chords are quite different from other ukuleles, and its size comparable to the guitar also makes it difficult to play.

Specifications

- Its scale length is 19 inches.
- Its overall length is 30 inches.
- Its common tuning is D-G-B-E.

Specialty Ukuleles

Specialty ukuleles also exist in addition to standard-sized ukuleles. These ukuleles are mostly formed in combination with some other instruments. If you want some variable instrument just for fun, then a specialty ukulele is the best choice, but if you are a beginner, then it is recommended to stick with standard ukuleles.

Banjoleles

Banjoleles like the Oscar Schmidt OUB-1 are just like the ukuleles in tuning as well as size, but they give you a strumming banjo tone because of their banjo styled body. A banjolele is a four, five, or six-string instrument.

Guitarleles

Guitarleles are six-string ukuleles, and they are tuned like a guitar. The best example is the Yamaha GL1. Guitar players do not need to learn this instrument because it is played just like a guitar, but it gives a sound like a ukulele. And it is a great chance for ukulele players as well to learn a guitar.

Recommendations

The type of ukulele which you should play depends on your choice and taste of music, and most often, your degree of practice and perfection in playing.

If you are a beginner to learn it, then you should go for a soprano ukulele or concert ukulele. These two ukuleles have a traditional sound that might be already inserted in your brain. Their size also makes them easy to play and to form chords.

If you are looking for a different sound and also love a piece of advance music, then you should stick to a tenor and baritone ukulele. It will sound good for you. While choosing a suitable ukulele, its size matters a lot. If you have small-sized hands then for your easiness you must think about the soprano and concert ukuleles. For bigger hands, the soprano and concert ukuleles are not comparable to the size of hands, and it might be difficult for you play them, so in this case, you must choose the ukulele of some larger size like tenor or baritone which would be agreeable for you.

But it does not matter what size you choose; it is up to you how you handle and play your ukulele

Chapter Six

Notes of the Ukulele

Referring to the piano keyboard is one of the best ways to play the notes and to know your ukulele better. Throughout this text, we will refer to the portions of the keyboard which relate to the ukulele. It would help you a lot if you can try the things you would be told on a keyboard. You can use any keyboard, be it an electronic keyboard or a piano, but if you don't have access to one, just go online and search for a piano simulator. Experiment on whichever simulated online keyboard works for you.

Creative Commons

Notes of Each String and How to Hold a G Chord

Musical Scales

The musical scales are the bases of all music, and among them, the C major scale is the most well-known and the easiest one. Only white keys of the piano are used to play the C major scale. C-D-E-F-G-A-B comprises the C scale. Usually, to the mentioned seven notes, a repeat of the C, which is the first note, is also included, which then becomes the number 8.

Any note of the keyboard can be transformed into a scale. Every one of these scales has specific patterns. One of those patterns is the major scales, and the other patterns are the minor scales. For our purposes, we don't need to know how the scales are formed. We just have to keep in mind that every scale has a specific order for the different patterns of notes. One or two black keys on the piano are used in other major scales; only the C major scale is the one that uses just the white keys.

You would see that each black key is mentioned with a # (sharp) and a b (flat). Depending on the scale you are in, you would have to call a specific black key a flat (b) or a sharp(#), but for the ukulele players, it is not important. Therefore, a black key between D and E can be addressed as a D# or an Eb. It doesn't matter what you call the black key, but it would matter if you started composing music.

When you are repeating the C major scale, make sure to include a repeat of the C which would become: C-D-E-F-G-A-B-C

There are also five more keys between the eight C major scales keys, and all of them are black. These are not included in the C major scale. Here these are mentioned as # (sharps): C-C#-D-D#-E-F-F#-G-G#-A-A#-B-C.

We will discuss one more major scale and then go to the ukulele. The G major scale also has one sharp key, which is the F#. Including the repeat of G, the eight notes of the G major scale are: G-A-B-C-D-E-F#-G

Notes on the Ukulele

All the flats and sharps are black, which makes it is easy to imagine the notes on a piano keyboard. If you would go and play on the keyboard by changing between the black and white notes, you would easily be able to distinguish between the sounds they produce.

The ukulele fretboard also contains the notes; those are just not as apparent as the ones you see on the piano. To understand the notes on the ukulele fretboard, let's compare the four strings of the ukulele with the piano keyboard.

With the standard-tuned G-C-E-A ukulele, the lowest note you can play is the middle C. C-E-G-A are the notes produced when you move from the lowest to the highest pitch. Still considering the order of strings, G-C-E-A is used to call the tuning of the standard ukulele.

In a piano, the black keys alternate in sets of 2s and 3s, just left of each set of black key sits the C key. The C middle is the C key, which is closest to the middle of the keyboard. The middle C is the lowest note you can play on the ukulele. Depending on the size of the ukulele, the highest note can change on the piano, but most commonly, it is 16 keys up from the middle C.

You can see that on the ukulele, you have a much narrower range as compared to a piano. Nevertheless, you can still play a lot of popular music on it.

Whole Steps and Half-Steps
Knowing the difference between the half and whole steps will help you understand your ukulele better. The interval between adjacent keys on a piano is referred to as half a step. The interval between the D and D# is also referred to as a half-step. As there is no black key between E and F, and B and C, the interval between them is another half-step. Two half-steps combine together to make a full step or a whole step. D#-F is another such full step or whole step, which comprises of two half-steps; D#-E and E-F.

There are also half-steps and whole steps on the ukulele; the half-step is the distance between 2 adjacent frets, and the whole step is made up of two half-steps.

With the information we have, now we can look at the ukulele fretboard closely. The note of a particular string such as G, C, E, or A is played by plucking the open string. A different note will be produced when you press down a fret (which means the space between the strips). Moving towards the soundhole, you will get a half-step higher between two adjacent frets. So if you pressed the A string's first fret, you would get an A# pressing the second fret of A string would give a B, and the third fret would give a C and so on. You would see that these notes are the same as the half-steps you would get on a piano.

If you were to label the first five frets on the fretboard it would be like this:

For G string: G#-A-A#-B-C (1st-2nd-3rd-4th-5th fret respectively)

For C string: C#-D-D#-E-F (1st-2nd-3rd-4th-5th fret respectively)

For E string: F-F#-G-G#-A (1st-2nd-3rd-4th-5th fret respectively)

For A string: A#-B-C-C#-D (1st-2nd-3rd-4th-5th fret respectively)

By comparing to the above mentioned, you would see that by pressing 1st fret of A string, we get A#, for 2nd fret of E string we get F#, for 3rd fret of C string we get D# and for 4th fret of G string we get B.

Remember and practice this for the above mentioned first five frets. Keep in mind that the distance between the adjacent frets is a half-step; two half-steps make a whole step. Experiment with these on the piano or the piano simulator, and you will be able to distinguish between the sounds, then try these notes on the ukulele and see if you can differentiate there as well.

Chapter Seven

Musical Keys and Chord Progressions

Each kind of music comes under some type of "key." The most famous songs usually come under one of these keys: A, C, D, and F. These keys contain the scale of notes which have the same name as them. For example, all of the chords of the F major scale will come under the key of F. The key of C will contain all of the chords of the C major scale, etc. More than one key can be used to write and play many different songs. Clementine is one such song that you can play in the key of F or key of C. Therefore, the choice of keys depends on the type of music you are playing.

Since specific chords come under specific keys, therefore the type of chords to be played in a certain song depends on the key. If a song is being sung in a key of C and you start playing the key of G, the performance would not sound correct. There is a huge difference between the key of C, and the key of G. F# is played in the key of G whereas the natural F note is played in the key of C. Thus, for a certain song to sound good, the same key should be sung and played by everyone.

There are many different ways, which can allow you to tell which key the song is in. Here we will only discuss two of them. First is the pretty obvious one, at the top of a chart of the song, the key of the song is usually written, e.g., next to the name of the song; the key of F which tells you the song is in key of F. The second is to look at the starting and the ending chords of the songs. So if a song started with a C chord and ended with a C, then the song would be in the key of C. There are times when the starting and the ending chords are different. When this situation arises, the key is determined by the last chord of the song.

Chord Transitions and C Major Scale's Chords

When three or more notes are played together, a chord is produced. As mentioned in the previous chapter, the C major scale contains the C, D, E, F, G, A, B, C, and the music, which is played in the key of C constitutes of the chords of this scale. Using any of the notes of this scale, you can create a 3-note chord. You can play up to seven 3-note chords with this scale. Of those seven, three are very important they are the C Major (1st), the F Major (4th) and the G Major (5th) chords. In most of the sources, you will find these addressed as "I" for the first (1), "IV" for the fourth (4), and "V" for the fifth (5).

Before we move on to the ukulele to learn these three chords, as told in the previous chapter here are the notes we get on the first five frets on the fretboard of the ukulele:

For G string: G#-A-A#-B-C (1st-2nd-3rd-4th-5th fret respectively)

For C string: C#-D-D#-E-F (1st-2nd-3rd-4th-5th fret respectively)

For E string: F-F#-G-G#-A (1st-2nd-3rd-4th-5th fret respectively)

For A string: A#-B-C-C#-D (1st-2nd-3rd-4th-5th fret respectively)

When you would hold the G string at the first fret and pluck it, you would get a G#. When you hold down the C string at the second fret and pluck that string, it will give you a D, and when you hold the A string at first fret and pluck that string, you get an A#, etc. It would help you a lot if you can remember the above mentioned first five frets. Also, remember the number of your fingers because, in some contexts, instead of the name of the finger, the number is used. Through index to pinkie finger, the fingers are numbered as 1, 2, 3, and 4.

Chord Transitions

Most of the time, you would be moving back and forth between I-IV-V (C Major, F major, G major, respectively) chords when playing music; this alternate movement is known as chord transition or chord progression. Because the sounds this transition makes are more delightful than others, this chord transition makes most of the popular music. The songwriters didn't suddenly decide that it was the best transition. They experimented with this and many other transitions. So, in the end, it is considered the best because it sounds better than other transitions and because it sounds better, it is played more frequently.

You will be able to play most of the songs if you know the I-IV-V transition for the most used keys.

Key of C I-IV-V Chord Transition

To play the I or the C chord, place your ring finger on the A string's third fret and then strum. What you will be playing is the G-C-E-C, not the G-C-E-A, because the A string is now playing the note C instead of A. The other strings are open so they would play the usual G, C, and E.

Before moving on to the G and F chords, let's see the difference between a piano chord and a ukulele chord. To play the different notes of a chord on a real piano, either you can use your three fingers simultaneously or play a broken chord. A broken chord is produced when you play each note one after the other, e.g., first C, then E, and lastly G. You can say that all ukulele chords are broken chords because when you strum, you can't hit every string at the same time. Nevertheless, both the ukulele and the piano would produce the same C-E-G chord. Before playing specific chords on the ukulele, you should play them on the piano because the piano makes the chords easy to understand.

For the key of C's F chord transition, place the index finger on the E string's first fret and place the middle finger on the G string's second fret. When you would strum this, you would play an A-C-F-A. The E string would give you an F at the first fret, and the G string would produce an A at the second fret. The C string and the A string are open, so they would give you a C and an A, respectively. So the F chord is made up of A-C-F-A.

To play the G chord or the "V" chord, hold down the C string at the second fret with your index finger, place the middle finger on the A string's second fret, and set the ring finger's fingertip on the E string's third fret. The strumming will give you D at the C string's second fret, G at the E string's third fret, and B at the A string's second fret. Altogether, you would be playing the F chord, which is made up of G-D-G-B.

The Key of G I-IV-V Chord Transitions
Now let us take a look at another key, which is just behind the key of C in terms of popularity, the key of G. On the piano, the G major scale comprises of the G-A-B-C-D-E-F#-G. When you compare it to C major, the G major also has a sharp in it; it's the F #.

We will now discuss the G major scale's I-IV-V chord transitions. As you can see from the above mentioned G major scale that the I (first) and the IV (fourth) chords of a G major scale are similar to V (fifth) and I (first) chords of the C major scale, they are the G and the C chords respectively. As these chords are the same, they are played in exactly the same way as mentioned above. Now what we are left with is the V (fifth) chord; it is the D chord (remember if the attribute of the chord is not mentioned, it means that chord is a major chord). To play the D chord, put your index finger on the G string, the middle finger on the C string and the ring finger on the E string, the fret for all of them is the second one. So now, when you would strum, you would be playing the D chord comprising of A-D-F#-A. The G string would give you an A. The C string would give you a D, and the E string would give you an F#. The A string is open, so it would give you an A.

Using V7 instead of V in Chord Transitions

Most of the time, when you are going through a ukulele book or a piece of printed music, you would find that "V7" is used as a substitution for the "V" chord in chord transitions. The V7 encompasses chords such as C7, F7, and G7, etc. these chords are known as the "seventh chords." You would find these chords often in popular music. When you are playing the I-IV-V chord transition, the V7 chords are mostly played instead of the V chords; this is an example of the chord substitution. Both of these chords are very similar to each other, but the V7 chords are given more preference.

Key of C Chords

You already know the chords of the C major scale. They are the C, Dm, Em, F, G, and Am. But when you use chord substitution, you play a G7 instead of G (which is the V chord in the I-IV-V chord transition). When a seventh cord is used, the basic 3-note gets one additional fourth note. When you use a G7 chord, you would be adding an extra note to the 3-note G-B-D of the G chord. The fourth note would be the F note. On the piano keyboard, a G7 is played as a G-B-D-F, you can see a fourth note F is added to the standard G chord.

On a ukulele, the G7 is played by putting the index finger on E string's first fret, the middle finger would go on the C string's second fret, and the ring finger would go on the A string's second fret. The open G string would play a G note, the C string would play D note at the second fret, the C string would play F note at the first fret, and the A string would play B note on the second fret. The major difference between G7 and G is that the G7 has an additional F note. The G chord only plays G, B, D notes, whereas the G7 plays G, B, D, and F note.

Key of F Chords

The F major scale is made up of F, Gm, Am, Bb, C, and Dm. But when you use chord substitution, the C7 chord is used instead of the C chord. On a piano, the C7 is played using the C, E, G, and Bb notes were as the C was played simply by using C, E, and G notes. The C7 adds the fourth note Bb (B flat) to the standard 3-note C chord.

On a ukulele, the C7 is played by placing the index finger on the A string's first fret. Strumming this will result in the production of G, C, E, and Bb notes. The G, C, and E strings are open, so they produce the usual G, C, and E notes. The A string would produce a Bb note at the first fret. You can see that the C chord only played G, C, and E notes, whereas the C7 chord has an additional note the Bb (B flat) note

Chapter Eight

UKE Fingerboard

Most of the beginner ukulele players are familiar with the most common four chords discussed in the previous chapter, the C, D, F, and G chords. Most players are still not familiar with the notes of the ukulele fretboard. To learn more about the ukulele, one must know about the notes on the different frets of the fretboard or should know how to find the note on a certain fret. I will keep this simple' if you don't learn the ukulele's fretboard, you cannot possibly understand how to play the ukulele the correct way. Here are all the notes on the ukulele fretboard.

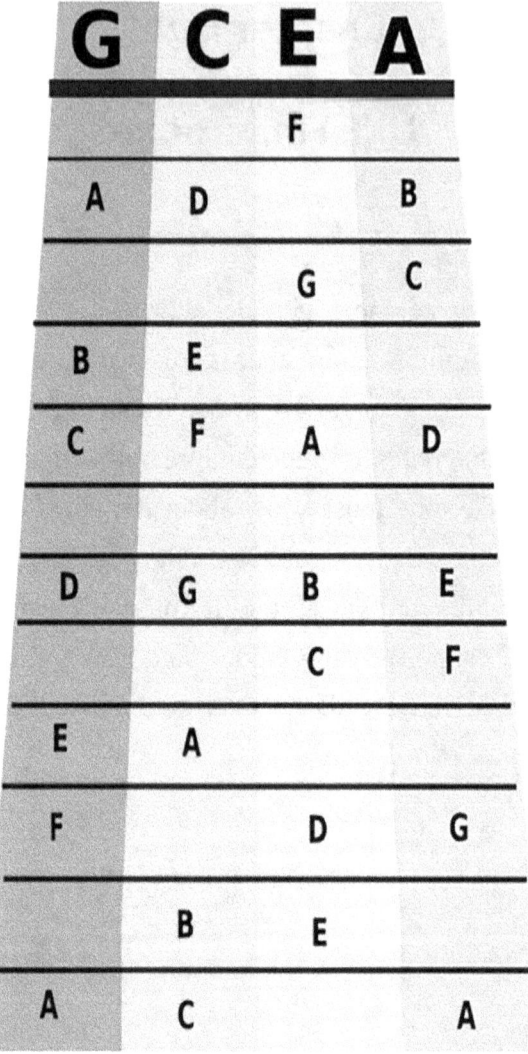

http://openclipart.org/detail/189182/ukulele-notes-by-bedpanner-189182

Ukulele Fingerboard

G string: G#, A, A #, B, C, C#, D, D#, E, F, F#, G, G#, A, A#, B (1st to 16th fret respectively)

C string: C#, D, D#, E, F, F#, G, G#, A, A#, B, C, C#, D, D#, E (1st to 16th fret respectively)

E string: F, F#, G, G#, A, A#, B, C, C#, D, D#, E, F, F#, G, G# (1st to 16th fret respectively)

A string: A#, B, C, C#, D, D#, E, F, F#, G, G#, A, A#, B, C, C# (1st to 16th fret respectively)

Remember, just over the top of the fretboard lies the nut. The fret which you would probably never use is the 16th fret, the last one. You might be thinking about how the notes mentioned above are played. Playing them is easy, but remembering them needs a little hard work. To play a specific note, place your fingertip on the fret of that note and pluck the string, you would get the required note. Let's say you want to produce a D note. Place the fingertip on the second note of the C string and pluck that string, you would get a D note. For an F note, you can put your finger on the first fret of the E string and pluck that string, etc. You can see we have used #'s, but in some places, you might see a b (flat); both of them represent the same notes, e.g., A# can be substituted with a Bb or an Ab can be used instead of G#, etc.

My advice is that you should at least learn the first five notes and then find ways to discover the others. You can easily find the next frets of the ukulele. They are just the same as the successive piano keys, also containing the black keys. You can say the notes are moving up one half-step. For a better understanding, let's discuss the piano's C major scale. The C major scale including the #'s (black keys) on a piano is like this: C, C#, D, D#, E, F, F#, G, G#, A, A#, B, C

Now let's look at some statements and verify them with the piano's C major scale and the notes on the ukulele.

- It's a half-step from C to C#, and the C string's first fret gives a C#.
- It's a half-step from C# to D, and the C string's second fret gives a D.
- It's a half-step from D to D#, and the C string's third fret gives a D#.
- It's a half-step from D# to E, and the C string's fourth gives an E.
- It's a half-step from E to F, and the C string's fifth fret gives an F.

When you look at all the notes of the ukulele, you might think, why is there not an E# or a B#? That is because there are no black keys on the piano between B and C and between E and F. Right now, you don't need to know the reason. Just memorize this fact that after B comes C and after E comes F. So if you have a note B on the ukulele's fretboard, you will find C on the next higher note on the same string; this makes C a half-step higher than note B. So if, on the ukulele's fretboard, you have a note E, the next higher note on the same string would be the note F. Thus it would be a half-step ahead of note E.

You can apply the same method to the other strings of the ukulele. Now let's look at the A string's first five notes and verify them with the piano's C major scale and the notes of the ukulele mentioned above.

- It's a half-step from A to A#, and the A string's first fret gives A# or Bb.
- It's a half-step from A# to B, and the A string's second fret gives B.
- It's a half-step from B to C, and the A string's third fret gives C.
- It's a half-step from C to C#, and the A string's fourth fret gives C#.
- It's a half-step from C# to D, and the A string's fifth fret gives D.

Do the same technique for the other strings first five frets. This way, you would be able to memorize these notes. And also, most of the songs are played on these first five frets notes.

When you have learned all the notes on the first five frets, try on your ukulele the C major scale which is C, D, E, F, G, A, B, C. When you look at the notes mentioned above on the ukulele fretboard, you see that the C major scale can be played in many different ways. The easiest way is to play the open strings together with the fretted strings. Defined below is a simple way by which you can play the C major scale on the ukulele fretboard.

- For the C note pluck the open C string
- For D place a finger on the C string's second fret and pluck
- For E pluck the open E string
- For F place a finger on the E string's first fret and pluck
- For G place a finger on E strings third fret and pluck
- For note A pluck the open A string
- For B place a finger on A string's second note
- For the repeat of the first note "C" (from the middle C, it's one octave higher), place a finger on A string's third fret and pluck.

Chapter Nine

Common Chords and Chord Substitutions

Below are mentioned some of the most played ukulele chords on the songs listed on the website known as the Ukulele Hunt. I advise you to learn as many of these chords as you can. In the beginning, chords like Bm and E might be too difficult and complicated for you to play. But fret not; chords substitutions are used to cater to these kinds of problems.

The chords are mentioned in the descending order of the number of times a certain chord has been played. The 20 most played chords are C, G, F, D, Am, A, Dm, Bb, D7, G7, Em, E7, A7, Bm, C7, B, E, Eb, Fm, and Gm.

In principle, you can play a specific chord in many different ways, so technically, it is possible to say that there are hundreds of chords. When you look for the C major chord, you will find 13 variations of it. It is quite amusing to go through them so you should visit the internet and go through all these variations. Despite this superabundance of the ukulele chords, if you learn a few other ukulele chords together with the 20 chords, which are mentioned above, you would become more than competent to play any song you encounter.

In the keys of C and G we have discussed up till now, you were told about the I-IV-V chord transitions. It appears that the chords in the transitions can be changed with one or more of the other ukulele chords. The chords are interchangeable because they have some kind of similarities. Usually, the chord which has been substituted is easier to play than the original one, and the substituted chord sounds just like the primary one.

Now we will discuss some of the common ukulele keys, their standard I-IV-V chord transitions, and the chords which can be used instead of the standard ones. You would come across cases where the standard chord is less popular than the substituted chord. Keep in mind that the keys discussed here are absolutely not all of the ukulele keys.

The ukulele key of C's I-IV-V chord transition consists of the C, F, and G (I-IV-V) chords. The first (I) or the C chord contains the notes C, E, and G. The chord CM7 and the C7 chord can be used instead of the C (I) chord. The F chord is the fourth (IV) chord, which is made up of F, A, and C notes. You can use the F7 chord as a substitute for the F chord. The G (V) chord includes the G, B, and D notes. The G7 chord can be used in place of the G chord.

The key of D's I-IV-V chord transitions is the D, G, and A chords, respectively. The first (I) or the chord D encompasses the D, F#, and A notes. You can use a D7 chord as a substitute for the D chord. The fourth (IV) chord is the G chord, which is made up of G, B, and D notes. The G7 chord can be used in place of the chord G.

The fifth chord is the A chord, it consists of A, C#, and E notes. Either Am or the A7 chord can be used instead of the chord A.

The I-IV-V chord transitions of the key of F are the F, A, and C chords, respectively. The F (I) chord is made up of the F, A, and C notes. The F7 can be used as a substitute for the F chord. The fourth is the A chord; it is comprised of the A, C#, and the E note. Both Am and A7 can be used as a replacement for the A chord. The fifth (V) chord is the C chord; it is composed of the C, E, and G notes. CM7 and C7 chords can be used in place of the C chord.

The I-IV-V chord transitions of the key of G are the G, C, and D chords, respectively. The G chord or the first (I) chord is constructed from the G, B, and D notes. The G7 chord can be used as a substitute for the G chord. The fourth (IV) chord, the C chord, is the combination of the C, E, and G note. The CM7 and C7 chords can be used instead of the C chord. The fifth chord is the E chord; it is made up of the D, F#, and A notes. The D7 chord can be used in place of the E7.

The I-IV-V chord transitions of the key of A are the A, D, and E chords, respectively. The first (I) chord A consists of the A, C#, and the E notes. Both Am and A7 can be used as an alternative to the A chord. The fourth (IV) chord, the D chord is made up of D, F#, and A notes. D7 can be used as a replacement for the D chord. The fifth (V) chord, the E chord, encompasses the G, B, and D notes. The E7 can be used as a substitute for the E chord.

After reading the above content, you might notice that the chords F7 and CM7 are not a part of the 20 most popular chords. Still, this doesn't make them difficult to play. To play an F7 chord, put your index finger on the E (2nd) string's first fret, the middle finger on the G (4th) string's second fret, and the ring finger on the C (3rd) string's third fret. By now, you might have noticed the similarities between the F7 and the F chord. To play the CM7 chord, put the middle finger on the A (1st) string's second fret and viola! You just made a CM7 or the Cmajor7 chord.

Chapter Ten

Lead Sheets, Sheet Music and Chords

You would see that the music played in ukulele club workshops are shown in either of the two ways. The first is the standard musical notation way, and the other is the song sheet one.

Standard Musical Notation

Things like measures (the section between two bar lines is known as a measure or a bar), and the actual notes are shown in the standard musical notation. On top of the measures, the chords would appear. This type of representation is called a lead sheet. The ukulele's standard musical notation would have everything a musician needs to play a song such as the key and the time signature and the treble clef. Now we will discuss how a song is represented in the standard musical notation.

The treble clef is a symbol that looks like a fancy G. On the piano musical sheets, the treble clef would show the notes that would be played by the right hand of the pianist. The bass clef indicates the note for the left hand. On a music sheet, you would see five lines which would have four spaces in between them together with the line and the spaces are called a musical staff.

The lines are named as E G B D F when moving from the bottom to the top line. Let's assume that a song is played in the key of F. How would we know from a music sheet that it is played in the key of F? As mentioned in one of the previous chapters, look for the starting and the ending chords. As the song is in the key of F, it would most probably start with an F chord and would definitely end with an F chord. The other way to know that the song is in the key of F is that you would find one b on the treble clef's third line. Because the b is on the third line, it would mean all the B notes would be flatted (b). Next to the b, you would find some numbers; these numbers represent the time signature. Let's say number 3 is written above 4; it would mean there would be three beats every measure, and one beat would be of one-quarter note.

To play the Ukulele using the standard musical notation, you just have to keep in mind the chord changes. There is no need to read the musical notes; you can just ignore all of them. You would find the chords written above the notes.

The one advantage the standard musical notation has over the other way, the song sheets, is that the standard one keeps all the players in accord, meaning everyone gets to play a song a similar way. The song sheets allows changes to be made according to the necessities of the group. When using the song sheets, occasionally the music is changed a bunch of times, so that some of the players can play the music in other keys. You probably won't find this thing happening when using the standard musical notation. Beloff Daily Ukulele books are quite popular; in these books, you would find the standard musical notation or the lead sheets for over 700 ukulele songs. These standard books are used in some of the ukulele groups, which actually results in keeping everyone on the same page.

Sheet Music

You now know what a lead sheet looks like. Let's revise it again; on a lead sheet, you would find the letters of the chords shown above the melody line. The song sheets don't have any melody lines consisting of the notes; they only have the letters for the chords and the lyrics of the song. As these are not standardized, these song sheets are, most of the time, modified to meet the necessities of the particular groups. Speaking from my experience, almost all the groups I have attended (for now, ten separate ones and still increasing) prefer the song sheets over the standard musical notation. The song sheets are less daunting as compared to the lead sheets, which would surely scare new players with all its notes and stuff. Most of the experienced players prefer song sheets because these can be easily modified to meet their demands.

Let's now discuss some of the songs in different keys. First, we will discuss a portion of the song "Clementine" written in the key of F. The portion we are discussing ends with the lyrics "Dreadful sorry Clementine." When a song is written in the key of F, its I-IV-V chord transition would be F, A, and C. When this portion of Clementine is shown in the key of F, it would only use the F and the C7 chords. C7 is used as a chord substitute for the C chord. Now let's say the same portion is shown on a song sheet in the key of C. The key of C's I-IV-V chord transitions are C, F, and G, respectively. The portion would only use the C, and G7 chords of the I-IV-V chord transition of the key of C. G7 are used as a substitute for the G chord. From this, you might get the idea that simple songs only use two of the three chords from the I-IV-V chord transitions.

Songs like "Five Foot Two" and "This Land" use all the chords of I-IV-V chord transitions. If "Five Foot Two" is written in the key of C, its I-IV-V (1st, 4th, and 5th respectively) chord transitions would be C, F, and G. These chords (with chords substitution) together with other chords, like E7, A7, and D7 would produce the song Five Foot Two. If the song "This Land" is shown on a song sheet in the key of G, it would use all the I-IV-V chord transitions of the key of G. Specifically, these chords would be G, C, and D7. D7 is used as a chord substitute for the D chord.

Chapter Eleven

Chord Vexation and Movable Chords

By now, you know a lot about the basics of how to play the Ukulele. The instrument is capable of generating some very interesting and attractive music, which is why knowing how to play it is to your advantage on any given day.

While we have looked over the simple aspects of playing notes and tones, it is time to move towards the more complex concept of changing chords. Many ukulele players have problems in changing chords while keeping the rhythm of their music intact. The process of changing chords is particularly complex because it can hurt the rhythm that you've built within your music. There are two very basic reasons why you might find it hard to change chords. Firstly, by now, you only know about playing single chords, and do not know what is required for changing chords up. Secondly, you can easily lose your rhythm in the process of changing chords. Both of these situations can be complex and hard for all ukulele players to go against. As a ukulele player, you need to make sure that the situation is under control, and you aren't making any errors in judgment.

Insufficient practice is also one of the reasons why changing chords can bedevil all uke players. Physical limitations and uncommon chords also come across as limitations, because it takes time for your fingers to adapt to the sudden reflex required for changing chords. Once you have adapted to the process, your fingers act upon reflex and muscle memory, which is why it is easier to follow up on these chords.

Physical Limitations

1 and 2 fret chords are easier for everyone to play. These chords require minimal action and don't challenge the movement of your fingers in any way possible. Three fret chords happen to be the most troublesome, as they require you to press strings across three different locations. These are more difficult than one or two chords and can put you in a lot of physical complications. The situation can be solved if the chords are located nearby each other on the uke. If the chords are nearby, you don't have to put in much effort, and can easily solve the problem. The fingers need to be close together to play the chords in the best manner possible.

There are 20 most popular chords played by uke players, out of which nine happen to be 3-fret, which just increases their importance. Moving on, out of the five most popular chords played by Uke players, two happen to be 3-fret. The G and the D are the two which happen to be 3-fret out of the five most popular chords.

The complexity level usually goes out of the charts with four-fret chords, which are a lot more difficult to pull out for uke players. These chords require expert handling, for which you have to be prepared at all times. These chords are generally more difficult to play because you have to play the strings from four different places. These are extremely difficult to handle, especially if you have to use just one finger on one or two frets. These barre chords are a hassle to manage for all uke players, as they have to move their fingers from chord to chord, contemplating the repercussions that come with all of them. Barre chords are extremely difficult for people to manage, as they give you the challenge of moving one finger across multiple chords at one time.

Four-fret chords are considered special in the world of uke players because they happen to be known as closed chords. By closed chords, we mean a string of chords, where there aren't any open strings present. These chords are also called movable chords and are a lot easier to manage for professionals. Experts suggest that they are called movable chords, as you have the option to move them up and down the fretboard, based on whatever you are more comfortable with. You can get a different chord whenever you please if you are particularly dissatisfied with the chord in context. Once you master the fingering of these 4-fret closed chords, you can easily get the desired results. Mastering the fingerings of just one barre chord can help you in mastering the fingerings for all of them.

Most beginners are found wanting when it comes to playing this chord. They find playing this chord the most difficult out of all the lot, as they do not really know how to include and play it within a song. This chord is important because it is considered movable and can easily be used within other chords to create magic of your own.

However, beginners need to note that this chord is movable and can easily be used to play other chords as well. As soon as you get the hang of the shape of these chords, you can move them up the board to play them differently.

There are going to be times when you will experience physically challenging chords. These chords do enhance the quality of the music being generated, but you have to realize that you need to innovate with alternatives whenever they appear. Yes, all of us are looking to get the best results possible from the uke, but you also have to know your limitations and what you can pull off. There are some physically challenging chords that you can never play, even while wanting. The best way to manage such chords is to skip over them and find a reasonable alternative. The alternative should give you a similar sound, without being as physically challenging as the one that you are about to change.

Uncommon Chords

There are well over a thousand possible combinations of chords that can be played on the ukulele. You need to realize which are uncommon, and which are common for you to play. Very experienced players of the ukulele would know many of these chords happen to be uncommon, and know just how they should go about tackling them. These professional players also know the chord placement and charts for over a hundred of these chords. Besides just knowing about these chords, experienced players can play these chords whenever the need be.

The issue arises when beginners are starting to learn these chords. Out of the thousand possible chord combinations, beginners should be lucky or happy to learn even a dozen of them. Many professional players carry single page chord charts with all relative details. These can appear extremely intimidating for the beginner level player, as they are just getting used to seeing all of this information, and what comes along with it.

Let's just say that you are a beginner and happen to know the G and the G7. Both of these chords happen to be present on the list for the 20 most popular chords by Ukulele Hunt. These chords are famous among professionals and beginners alike. A chord chart for the letter G will contain intimidating sets of information about how the chord can be elongated into a beautiful rhythm. You don't really have to know or memorize this information. In fact, we are sure that many professional players do not even know half the information that comes within these single chord charts. Not many uke players know about letter charts, which is why they carry them around. As a beginner, there is no need for you to get intimidated or overwhelmed by these charts.

Every ukulele playing session that you participate in will have a mention of chords that you have never heard before. While playing or hearing these chords, you need to make sure that you know what they translate into. Even if you think you know the chords that come as part of every section, you have to make sure that you are ready to play the uncommon chords.

Even if you know all common chords within a ukulele set, you can consider yourself a decent player of the equipment. Regardless of just how much you know about common chords, there are going to be uncommon chords like B7, G6, and Edim, which would scare the living life out of you. You might know what these chords mean, but you won't know them enough to transition towards success with them quickly. Uncommon chords crop up all the time, and it can be easy for you to get overwhelmed by them. However, whenever uncommon chords pop up, you need to be ready to play something that can act as an alternative. Whenever an uncommon chord pops up, you should either play an alternative or should look to play something that is similar to the initial chord. For instance, if you have to play a Gmaj7, which is an uncommon chord, you can substitute it by playing the G, which is a common chord. This simple substitution would save you the hassle of disrupting your rhythm or changing the meaning of the music.

It is okay for even professionals not to know all the chords. No one knows all the chords that go into making music. But what you need to know is just all that goes into making your music better. You should be able to make decisions in the heat of things. As a professional player, you need to know the importance of not letting uncommon chords come in between what you are looking to achieve. Uncommon chords shouldn't deter you from your goals and objectives, and should instead help you achieve them. Find your way through uncommon chords, by using your information of them and playing something similar.

Chapter Twelve

Chord Tricks

As you gain experience as a ukulele player, you are going to encounter multiple tricks and techniques on your way. There are a significant number of tricks that ukulele players can learn from. When you start learning the ukulele for the first time, you aren't going to have sufficient expertise in playing the equipment. They say practice makes a man perfect, and that is exactly what applies when you are learning how to play the ukulele. Practice is what will make you perfect, and practice is just what you have to do.

When we talk about tricks, there are numerous tricks and techniques that ukulele players can try at any given time. These tricks are meant to make playing the uke easier for you and help you become the best at what you are currently. These tricks involve different chords, which is why you have to be an expert at playing them if you really do want to succeed.

The more experienced you are as a ukulele player, the better positioned you will be to play these tricks in the best manner possible. When talking about tricks, we mean short cuts, chord substitutions, different fingerings, and a lot more different techniques. All of these techniques make it easier for you to play the ukulele and help you get the best out of the equipment.

As a beginner, when you are starting to play the ukulele for the first time, you should educate yourself about these tricks there and then. All short cuts and chord substitutions are meant to make playing the equipment a lot easier for you. You can easily jump from chord to chord, without worrying about losing your rhythm or anything else. The good thing about this is that you can easily play the chord to perfection through substitution methods. These techniques help make it easier for you to play the ukulele, without losing out on the quality of the rhythm being played.

In this chapter, we mention some of the best uke chord tricks for you to pull. Before we mention them, you should know the pertinent and relevant finger names for your different fingers. The numbers allotted to fingers would hold true for the fingers of your fretting hand. It is best for you to take the entire process seriously, and recognize the fingers that need to get the job. Finger number 1 is used to refer to your index finger, while finger number 2 is used to refer to your middle finger. Finger number 3 is used to refer to your ring finger, and finger 4 is used to refer to your pinkie. You don't use the thumb for playing the ukulele, which is why you don't have to worry about the thumb being allotted a number or not.

Tonally Similar Chords

While playing the ukulele, you will come across many chords which are different from one another but are tonally similar in the music that they produce. These chords can be substituted with each other, because they have a similar impact, without requiring you to flex your hands or fingers a lot.

C Major 7 for C Major

The C major 7 or C7 chord can sometimes be substituted for the C major chord because they happen to be tonally similar. All of these chords can be used together, as you will get similar results out of them. The C major chord is similar to the C7 chord, as it gives the same tone as the C7 chord. This means that you can interchangeably use both of these chords in the best manner possible. The results you get will be in your best favor and will help you get the best results possible.

If we consider the advantages of doing so, there are no major advantages of changing majors up. There is no advantage with substituting the C7 with the C major, but it allows you to mix things up a bit. Playing the C is considered necessary for success as a ukulele player, which is why it is simpler for you to manage and play these chords. You need to realize the importance of substituting chords in the required situation. Chords shouldn't be substituted out of place, and you should only substitute them when the need be. Substituting the chords without any prior notice can be a bit uncalled for.

D7 for D

Just like you can substitute the C chords, you can also substitute the chords within D. The substitution can help make playing the uke easier for you, and allow you to get a tonally similar alternative to what you are already playing. The D7 chord can be substituted for D in many songs that you play. The D7 chord happens to be extremely similar to the D chord in many songs, and the substitution allows you to play both these chords interchangeably. The best part about doing so is that you can get the desired results possible from your chord placement.

There is, however, a minor difference when it comes to substituting both of these chords. The difference is that D7 adds another note to the D chord, which is known as C. The fourth note added to the chord, adds a lot of difficulties. All beginners will now be right to ask, just how can a D7 be easier to play than a D? Well, if we look at playing styles, a D7 isn't easier to play than a D. However, a substitute for the D7 is easier for you to play than the D. Since both of them can be used interchangeably, you can play a D7 whenever you see a D in the notes. This gives you the option to simplify the notes for you and make sure that you are physically able to play the notes, without having to jump towards a fourth C note.

E7 for E

Following the chord tricks in C and D, you can also substitute chords in the notes played for E. You can easily substitute the E7 for E because both of them make similar tones. We all know how difficult it can be to play the E chord. Regardless of whether you are a professional or a novice, you will know just how difficult it can be for you to play the E chord. Playing the E chord can be a bit difficult for all professionals, as you have the press the C, G, and E strings present on the 4th fret. Plus, you also have to press the A string on the 2nd fret. Playing all these notes can eventually be physically challenging, as there is no way you will be able to manage the load that comes with them. So, if you are somewhere around the key of A, you can easily substitute an E7 for an E. The tones sound extremely similar, which is why you don't have to worry about the sound coming out wrong or anything.

You can also try this substitution with other keys as well. You can get away with the substitution if everything goes as planned. However, you will have to check whether the sound is coming out right or not. You cannot just go about playing the chords without having checked the tones that come out first. Whenever you plan to use a substitute in a performance, it is best first to practice it to see whether they have a similar tone or not. If the tones are almost similar, then you can proceed with getting the change done.

Same Name, Different Notes

This is a very rare situation and is not something that you will normally encounter or see. To be honest, D7 is the only time you are going to encounter the situation of the same chord name but different notes. Anyone who has played the D7 chord will know that it involves pressing the D, F, A, C notes. The notes are easy to remember, but there are two different finger patterns that you can follow for playing this chord. Both of these finger patterns produce the same name and lead to similar results. You can find one or another of these patterns listed down in chord charts and books. One of the patterns used for playing the D7 is the Hawaiian pattern and is easier to manage. This pattern is called the Hawaiian D7 and is present within all books and chord notes alike. You are strumming different notes along the lines of D, F, A, C when you are playing the pattern.

Interestingly, the Hawaiian D7 leaves out the major D note and only plays the 3 D7 notes within the chord. All beginners are forced to ask whether this is a permissible way to play the D7 note. To answer this question, well, yes, it is. In this particular instance, when you are playing the D7 without D notes, the sound that is generated by your ukulele is almost similar to what is generated when all of these notes are being played together. So, substitution in this instance is not just permissible but is also recommended to all beginners and experts alike. Beginners have difficulty playing specific chords, which is why they are motivated to use these tricks and chords.

A dominant 7 chord is easy to identify for beginners. Anytime you see a note letter followed by the number 7, you can tell that it is a dominant 7 chord. All C7, D7, and F7 notes are dominant 7 chords.

Same Exact Chord, Alternate Fingering

Moving in with the tricks you can apply while playing the ukulele, we now talk about playing the same exact chord, but with alternative fingering. Almost all of the chords that you see being played can be fingered with different patterns. This is something that almost all beginners identify when they start playing the significant sevens on the fretboard. The dynamics of the fretboard allow players to play the numbers in different ways.

To give you some perspective, professional players of the Ukulele can play the D7 chord in eight different ways. All of these eight different ways require different finger placements and advanced attention to detail. You have to make sure that you follow these finger placements to the T and achieve the perfect alternative techniques.

Most beginners can have a hard time playing the D7 higher up on the fretboard. Even players with some experience can have trouble playing the D7 when it is located higher up on the fretboard. We realize how beginners are looking for ways to simplify the entire experience. You want alternate fingering patterns, which are easier to achieve and play. We mention two examples illustrating alternative methods of fingering, which can help you get the desired results from the process.

Playing E Minor from G Chord

The first example we will talk about is that of playing E minor from G chord with just one finger. Most beginners have issues following chord progressing from the notes of G to E minor. This requires lifting fingers, which we try to demonstrate here isn't necessary. You don't have to lift your fingers for playing the E minor when you are progressing from the G chord. The downtime can be troubling and can lead to a gradual slowing down of your results.

If you're playing the G chord, you can easily skip traditional fingering methods to play the E minor through your pinkie. Obviously, you need to have full trust in your pinkie, as this technique requires attention to detail and full command over what you are playing. Jumping from the G chord to E minor is hard, which is why your pinkie needs to be positioned at the C string, fourth fret. This fingering is known to work magic on all kinds of performances. Pressing the fret upwards of the keyboard helps in overriding any of the frets going down the keyboard. So, when you press the fourth fret located on the C string, you cancel the impact of your finger on the 2nd fret of C. This cancellation of the 2nd fret of the C string helps create the sound of the E minor chord. So, just by using your pinkie to good effect, you have created an amazing version of the E minor chord.

Moving Quickly From G to G7

The second example we are going to discuss is that of moving quickly from G to G7. Both G and the G7 chord are located adjacent to one another in almost all songs. The song sheet for *Let Me Call You Sweetheart* comes to mind, as both these chords are positioned close in this chord sheet as well.

If you follow the traditional fingering methods, you will have to lift not one, not two, but three different fingers to go from G to G7. The same will also apply when you are shifting back from one G7 to a G. However, you can position your fingers in such a way that it kills out the need for going back and forth. There is an alternative fingering method that allows you to easily go back and forth these notes without requiring significant effort.

You can create G notes by positioning your hand and fingers in the following manner:

- Position your middle finger on the 2nd fret of the C string
- Position your index finger on the 1st fret of E string
- Position your pinkie on the 3rd fret of the E string
- Position your ring finger on the 2nd fret of the A string

Once you have achieved this position, you can easily play G and G7 without any further hassle. When you lift your pinkie, you have a G7 chord being played. When you put your pinkie back down, you have a G chord being played. This allows you a certain amount of freedom while playing the ukulele and gives you exactly what you are looking for. You need to make sure that the process doesn't impact you much so that you can play music without a break.

Same Exact Fingering with Different Names

There are certain modifications that allow you to give different names to the same exact type of fingering style. Ukuleles that come with standard tuning mechanisms, including G, C, E, and A, will play chords C6 and Am7.

This is because all the G, C, E, and A are notes located within the C major scale. The C major scale, if you don't recall properly, includes all white keys on the piano beginning from C. This includes C, D, E, F, G, A, B, C. The relative minor for the C major scale was called the A minor scale, which included white keys on the piano starting from A. The keys here include A, B, C, D, E, F, G, A. There are no sharps or flats in either of these chords, as they have the same key signature. The chords for A minor 7 and C6 thus, have the same notes, but within a different sequence on the piano. So, if we looked at both these notes in musical terms, then C6 would be an inversion of A minor 7, and A minor 7 would be an inversion of C6. Strumming the Ukulele is an important practice and requires significant practice, so when you are strumming, all the strings located within are considered open, and you strum G-C-E-A. These four notes form the pattern for both A minor 7 and C6

Chapter Thirteen

Strumming

As of yet, we have only mentioned strumming briefly within this book. Strumming is an important technique for getting the best out of your ukulele routine. Strumming like an expert requires a lot of knowledge and inherent info about what strumming actually is. This chapter aims to build upon that info and strives to make you an expert at strumming on a ukulele.

We also haven't discussed any of the techniques you can follow for strumming as an expert. When you start as a beginner, you will realize that strumming can help you achieve a lot of diverse possibilities on the ukulele. This is because strumming comes with amazing variety and results. Beginners learning how to play the uke can practice strumming to do a basic downbeat strum in 4/4 or ¾ time. To master the strum, you need to show and practice a lot of skill and rhythm. Rhythm is extremely necessary for strumming because it is the rhythm you build that will eventually help you get the laurels that you are looking for from strumming. Practice is necessary because building rhythm isn't an easy job. Expert players can vary the strum from song to song without disturbing the rhythm. Being able to vary the level of strumming, without disturbing the rhythm is the highest pinnacle of strumming.

What fingers do you actually use for strumming? Some experts are more comfortable with using their index finger because it allows more variety in excellent rhythms. Beginners, on the contrary, like to use their thumb. The thumb does achieve the objective at hand but isn't the only digit you should use for strumming. You can expect and generate better results when you are strumming with your index fingers. When strumming with the index finger, you need to strum down using the nail of your finger. Playing the uke requires practice, expertise, and long nails, so you have to make sure you have all three. When you are strumming with your index finger, you have to make sure that you go down using the nail on your index finger. Once you have gone down, you can then go up using the fleshy part of your fingertip. This movement can help give you the kind of results you want and will deliver optimal results in no time. There are numerous videos and guides available online which help you learn how to strum as a beginner. Strumming is particularly tricky for beginners, which is why you have to find a way to learn it to get the kind of results you are expecting from the routine.

Having answered the question of which finger you should use for strumming, we now move on to the question of where exactly should you strum. To answer this question in a simplified manner, you should strum on whatever part of the board you know will give the best sound quality. Sound quality is the primary objective of all players when it comes to strumming, which is why they are really particular about which part of the fretboard to strum over to achieve the best sound quality. If you have a concert ukulele or a soprano, the best part of the fretboard is where the neck of your ukulele hits the body. The conduit between both of these solid structures is where you can find the best sound quality. Once you find the sweet spot, you can expect the best results in no time. Just hit the play button and get the most amazing sounds from your ukulele board.

Now, since we are discussing every facet of strumming here, we will also take a look at just what you need to do for strumming on tenor ukes. Tenor ukes have a different mechanism for strumming, and you should know just how to hit the bull's eye with these ukes. We believe that tenor ukes have their best spot further towards the nut. The area around the 12th fret is most melodious when it comes to tenor ukes, which is why you should play the pattern accordingly on your specific instrument.

Having discussed the finger to use for strumming and the best part of the fretboard to practice strumming on, we will now go on to discuss the next most important topic related to strumming; strum patterns. Strum patterns are necessary for acing the strumming routine, as they give you a sense of direction and results. However, before we jump into strum patterns, it is just as important to discuss the mechanics involved within an individual strum. Individual strums should be aced before you head on to patterns because perfection over a series of individual strums is what leads to the eventual success of a pattern. There are plenty of resources available on the internet, which helps you decide the best strumming pattern going forward and assist you with building the best individual notes.

Moving on to what is required for perfecting an individual strum, we take inspiration from a renowned uke player, James Hill. Hill has plenty of resources online and has summed his ideas brilliantly within videos and guides. These guides are meant to help people out with what is required for achieving the perfect strum.

Hill breaks the process of strumming down into four components, which he believes are equally essential to the process:

1. **Posture**: The posture you maintain while strumming is just as important as the actual routine you are following. By posture, we mean the shape of your hands as you strum your way to success. Your hands should ideally be placed in the best manner possible so that you can ace the pattern and the individual strum.

2. **The Path**: Secondly, you need to perfect the path your hands follow when they go past the strings. Your hands follow a definite path while going through the strings, which is why you must perfect that to achieve a good strum.

3. **Position**: Position is just as important as the two metrics mentioned above. In fact, if we break down each component according to the impact they have on the end result, we believe that the position where your hands end up making contact with the strings can be an even important metric. The position is important for getting the best sound quality from the strum you are about to create. Sound quality is

important and is a metric that you wouldn't want to mess up.

4. **Pressure**: Finally, the fourth most important metric for defining the success of the strum is pressure. Press can mean many things here, but in the context of strumming, it means the force you put into the strum. The pressure behind the strum needs to be excellent so that you can get the best results possible. Pressure in just the right amount is perfect for success, as anything more or less can wreck your pattern over.

You can watch videos online to see just how individual strumming works because more words wouldn't do much justice to what it takes for perfecting your strumming routine.

Strumming Patterns

Having discussed what is required for perfecting your individual strums, we now move to discuss strumming patterns and just how you can perfect them successfully. There are plenty of patterns available on the internet, but we have shortlisted five patterns, which will help you build upon your success as a beginner.

Beginners need to understand just how strumming works, as it is difficult for them to perfect the art without doing so.

Strumming Pattern #1

This strumming pattern is ideal for beginners to get started with, as it is easy to play and memorize on the fretboard. There is no complexity involved within this pattern, as you can easily play the ukulele with this pattern as well.

This pattern is a simple d-d-d-d in 4/4 time. You can also play this pattern in ¾ time, but then it would be considered as three down-strums in one measure of music. The pattern is simple to play and easy for beginners to understand as well. Experts say that you can further simplify this pattern by playing it across the C chord. Practicing strumming on the C chord can help you get the desired results.

Strumming Pattern 2

Strumming pattern 2 is the second most popular strumming pattern available in the market. The strumming pattern follows a definite movement across the fretboard, which is why you won't waste time remembering just what kind of movement is required from you. You should note that every down-up in this strumming pattern takes up just the same amount of time as a down-up in the strumming pattern number 1.

To help you understand the first two strumming patterns in even more detail, we take a look at how they will be played when playing an actual song on the uke. Below we look at what is required of you when playing the simple Hot Cross Buns melody through these strumming patterns. The melody is to be played in the G key. Chords for the melody are to be altered between G and D, and the song is to be played on 4 beats to the measure, or in a time sequence of 4/4.

Using the methods identified in Strumming Pattern#1, you will play the song in the following manner:

- 4 down strums in the first measure
- 4 down strums in the 2nd Measure
- 4 down strums on the 3rd measure
- 4 down strums on the 4th Measure

Using this pattern, you will be able to strum the melody for Hot Cross Buns through the strumming pattern number 1. Strumming Pattern number 2 is almost the same as the strumming pattern above, with the only difference being that the down strum is now a down-up strum. You use your strumming finger to hit the string only four times during the first pattern, but in the second pattern, you follow the same movement for over eight times.

You should keep practicing these patterns until you become more comfortable with what is happening around you. The strumming patterns to follow are basically a continuation of all that you have practiced within these patterns. Continuous practicing of patterns 1 and 2 would prepare you for the three patterns to come.

Strumming Pattern 3

This strumming pattern combines what you might have practiced in the first two patterns. This is a combination of both the first and the second strumming patterns. You start with a down, then move to down-up, then do a repeat down, and then perform another down-up to finish the movement. In short, you will be brushing the strings six times within one measure during this pattern. However, since it is a combination of both down and down-up movements, you would want some practice before you can master this pattern.

Strumming Pattern 4

Since every pattern in this list is a continuation of the previous pattern, strumming pattern 4 also builds on what you practiced and learned in strumming pattern 3 to rearrange the movements per measure. This pattern also requires six brushes of the string during one musical measure, but this time around, you have to mix up what you learned in the pattern before. In this pattern, you will be starting with a down-up than a down. The pattern goes down-up followed by a down, then down-up, and then another down. Having practiced pattern 3, this will be easier for you.

Strumming Pattern 5

This strumming pattern is also known as the calypso strumming pattern and is particularly tricky to master. The strumming pattern has been used in many popular videos and is still a fan favorite for many across the globe. You can see this strumming pattern used within popular songs such as The Sloop John B, Yellow, Day-O, Jamaica Farewell, Maryanne, and He's Got the Whole World in His Hands, among others. This pattern requires extensive practice, as you cannot ace it without regular practice. Regular practice is a must, as it helps you in building the right pattern for acing this music. This pattern requires practice because it has two continuous 'and up's following a down. This is different from all previous patterns and will require you to reconfigure your understanding of patterns and start fresh.

Strumming from Sheet Music

Strumming patterns can easily be understood when you have musical notations and in-depth details of measures to help you through them. But almost all uke groups have song sheets, which are used for displaying only words and chords. These song sheets can be complex to understand for most beginners, as you don't realize where measures begin and end. With your limited knowledge of measures and how they are shown in song sheets, you can easily mess up the information. As a general rule of thumb, you should follow the chords sung by the singer or another bass player. Following rhythm can help you perform well, whereas you can change chords whenever and wherever notified by the lyrics.

Practice is again a key aspect here, as you need to ensure you are in rhythm and sync with the rest of the singers and other players. Follow the tone set by the singer and the other bass players, so that you can keep the rhythm intact. Clearly following the rhythm helps increase the perfection of your music, while making it easier for every member to follow the lead of others.

Strumming and Rhythm

While all of the techniques and information are relevant and important, we believe you must complement the knowledge you have gained within this chapter with what is present on the internet.

There are plenty of informational videos available online, which will build upon you the importance of strumming rhythmically. To delve into this topic further, we help sum up the information in this chapter as a reminder for you.

Remember that strumming doesn't necessarily have to be a hard job for you to manage. As a beginner level player, you can start practicing strumming just like all other aspects of playing the ukulele. You do not have to create a master plan for tackling strumming, as you can practice what we have written here, with your routine uke playing routine. For now, you can revise the concepts in an enhanced manner within the info below.

The finger you use for strumming is ideally up to you. Beginners are more prone to use their thumb, but experienced players like using their index finger. You should go for whichever option you feel comfortable with, and shouldn't force yourself into anything. Remember that you have to use the nail on your finger of choice while going up, while you can use the tender flesh under the nail when you are coming down. This routine will make strumming on the uke extremely simple for you. Also, make room for experimentations whenever you are learning how to strum. Make sure that you know where and how to experiment. Experimentations are a must, as they teach you the correct pattern for handling the strumming routine. Without experimentations, you wouldn't be able to reach the desired results on the Uke board. You can also use a pick for strumming if you aren't able to use your fingers upfront. The pick doesn't have to be of hard plastic, like the one used for guitar, but you can use a soft pick for strumming on the uke. Detractors might say that using a pick will spoil your habits, but there is nothing wrong with utilizing a soft pick for strumming if you aren't comfortable with playing with your fingertips.

You need to know the best spot on the uke to strum on. On traditional ukes and sopranos, the best place to strum on is near the connection between the neck and the base of the ukulele. This is where the sound coming out is considered to be of high quality. You can utilize this space to good effect by strumming on that part of the fretboard. Additionally, you have to make sure that the rhythm is practiced before you step in for a performance. Practice the rhythm with your group and see whether the sound from that specific part is complementing the music you are about to create.

When you are playing within a group, you must keep strumming if you lose the rhythm or your place during a chord change. Keeping intact with the rhythm is more important than worrying about how to change the chord when you have lost pace with it. Strumming allows you to keep pace with the rhythm of the music being played, without letting anyone notice that you missed the ever-important chord change during the performance. We cannot overemphasize this point, because of how important it is. You must keep strumming and keep the rhythm intact whenever your performance is disturbed by a chord change you weren't able to keep up with. Beginners would want to know just which chord they should strum on if they lost the chord change. To answer this, you should strum on the basic chord the key currently is in. For instance, if the key is of C, and you fumbled trying to transition to an F7, then you should strum on the C key until you can get back on track. This will help save your performance and would make sure that your rhythm is on point without any hiccups as such.

As a beginner, you also need to practice in moderation when you are going to learn strumming patterns. Strumming patterns shouldn't be approached hastily, as you would want to take your time in approaching them. For starters, you should look to go one step at a time, rather than taking all strums by the scruff of the neck. Work on the first two patterns mentioned in this chapter initially, and make sure that you have completely mastered them before you jump to any other pattern. Strumming should ideally be done without any hiccups if you practice the patterns according to their difficulty level. You start with the first two and only move to the next two when you have mastered them. As soon as you have a certain level of proficiency over the first two, you can move over to the third and fourth ones. Once you fully capitalize on the third and fourth tones, you can then move on to the final calypso, which is also the hardest.

Learning patterns for strumming and mastering the techniques can be a complex task; however, going from one step to another in a gradual manner can make the entire process a lot easier. The information presented in this chapter will get you started for what is to come in the world of strumming, and how you can master it.

Chapter Fourteen

Playing Melodies on the Ukulele

All popular music we see around us is made up of harmonies and melodies. These melodies and harmonies are responsible for adding weight to the music and do a basic job at making sure that the music sounds melodious to the ears.

For starters, harmony is what we play and hear when the chords are strummed. Melody, on the contrary, is the sequence of notes present within the standard music notation. This sequence of notes is played on the treble clef and is used for producing melodies. However, the standard notion for playing music isn't popularly used in many of the uke jam sessions that we see around us. The standard notation for music carries a note of all melodies and harmonies, but that isn't followed when you are playing the uke. Playing the uke requires special consideration, as the music sheets used for playing it contain only words and chords. Uke players use song sheets instead of standard musical notation. Thus, considering the lack of proper information, the uke player is tasked to create the melody.

Melody is necessary within a tune, as that is what makes it more tuneful. It is the reason why we like singing specific songs such as Clementine, You are my Sunshine, and the Land is Your Land because we like the melodies that come with this music. The chords that come with these songs provide us with the right harmony and make the songs even more interesting and pleasant to listen to. As we have previously discussed within this book as well, the chord progression is used as the melody for many popular songs played with the ukulele.

Playing a Melody on the Ukulele

The ukulele is among the few instruments which can be used for playing melodies and chords. The melody for the ukulele is, however, somewhat embedded within the chords that come for the instrument. Every chord that is used for playing the ukulele comes with a separate melody note. To elaborate this information further, we can take the example of the Clementine, where the F chord has an F melody note, and the C7 chord has a G melody note.

When you strum the chords C7 and F along with the rhythm for a song, you don't hear the melody in your ears, because it is basically a couple of chords going back and forth. However, the melody happens to stand out when there are more chords involved within a song. The City of New Orleans is an example of a song that stands out because there are two melodies within that song. Once you play all the chords from the first four lines of this song, you will notice all of the melodies coming in order together and creating the required magic.

While all of the chords for uke players are responsible for incorporating the melody of any song, you still have to pick melody notes located within the treble clef. You can play 24 different notes in just the first five frets. The lowest note for the first five frets would lie on the C string, the middle C of the piano. The highest note for these five frets is the D, which can be played by pressing the A string. You can check this out for each note on your ukulele using a tuner. You must become accustomed to all of the notes present on the fretboard, in particular those which are used within the first five frets. The first line of the song, Clementine, can easily be played by just the notes on the treble clef.

When you are playing the ukulele during jamming sessions, you will find it hard to hear the melody of the uke audibly. This can happen because of several reasons. First of all, many beginner-level ukulele players don't have the skill set required for playing the melody at the speed of which songs are played or sung. They are incapable of keeping up with the speed, and eventually, end up losing the momentum that they have gained. The lowest note located on the standard ukulele is the middle C. However, many of the popular songs we see around us have notes lying down and below middle C.

Besides playing accurate notes, you also have to consider the rhythm that goes into music. There are four distinct and different note durations within the Clementine music; these durations include the half, quarter, eighth, and sixteenth notes. So, besides just plucking their notes right, the player also has to apply perfect and accurate note durations. This can end up making the melody even more difficult for all involved.

The sound for the ukulele doesn't carry really well in comparison to the guitar, which is why the sound is all drowned out by the strumming around it. These are just some of the reasons why you aren't able to identify melody when you play the ukulele in a jamming session.

However, even with all the melodies being drowned out in a jamming session, there are several reasons why you should learn to play melodies on the ukulele. Firstly, playing melodies helps teach you exactly where the notes are located on your fretboard. Playing melodies opens up the opportunity for you to pick the chords instead of practicing strumming. The resulting melody created when you pick notes individually from a chord can greatly enhance the beauty of a song. While jamming sessions with the ukulele hardly record a melody, your mel9ody will be appreciated and clapped upon during smaller group sessions, where it will be audible.

Also, when you are practicing alone, playing melodies is a lot more interesting and simpler than just strumming. Since you can experiment as much as you want when playing alone, you can also mix chord strumming with melody in multiple ways. You can also learn ukulele tablature by learning melody in its purest form.

Options to Play Melody
You have plenty of options to play a melody on the ukulele. All of these options happen to make the process easier and more manageable for you. There are three methods you can choose from

when learning how to play the ukulele. These methods to choose from include:

Play by Ear

This is the first and most comprehensive method of playing the melody as a ukulele player. In this method, you need to be seriously aware of the notes on the fretboard and need to have the melody embedded in your head. The location of the notes on the fretboard can let you know just how to add melody to the song. Additionally, knowing the melodies in your head can help you react to the needs of the song as it progresses. If you know how to do all of this without any trouble, then you are an already accomplished ukulele player, far beyond the kind of beginners this book is written for.

Read the Music

If you can't play the melody by your ears, you need to learn just how to read music from a sheet of standard music notation. The notes, pitch, and duration for the Clementine music are positioned on the treble staff. Knowing how to read music can simplify this entire process for you. You don't have to follow any undue protocols or processes if you know what is required of you while reading music. Reading music allows you to predict patterns and reach the due conclusion of what is best for you. Reading music can help you out with other musical equipment as well, besides the ukulele. Knowing how to do so is fairly helpful and gives you the desired outcome.

Read Tablature

Tablature is a simplified and easier way of finding and playing melodies. This is also the most recommended and preferred method by and for ukulele players. The tablature is meant to help you identify where to put your fingers and on which string. The tablature helps you find direction and melodies when you are learning how to play the ukulele. It contains specific instructions on just how you can ace melody. There are four lines in a basic table, which are aligned to form the ukulele as if it is in front of you. Once you get this in your head, you can get on your way towards playing tabs and melodies in the best manner possible.

Playing Durations on Tablature

While many artists prefer tablatures, there is a slight problem with them. The problem is that the duration of the notes or the melodies is not indicated within the tablature. The tablature shows you the pitch of the notes, but nothing more than that. This limited info isn't of much help at times, and you have to think of new ways to get the job done. The pitch of the note does not tell you anything about what is needed for durations.

So, how do you go around this conundrum to play music in the best manner possible? The best way to do so is through the following means:

Learn to Read Durations

Even if you do not read music and haven't learned to do so yet, you can always learn to read signatures and the time duration that they carry. When you start reading music, you will find it to be a lot easier than actually reading musical pitches as they come your way. Reading these pitches can be a lot easier for everyone involved.

While you might find it confusing at first, learning to read the note durations is in your best interest and can make playing music a lot easier for you. The tablature notes become fairly obvious when you read them in this manner. You can also start properly referring to durations, without any errors as such.

Play Melodies Based on Your Knowledge of the Song

The second way to guess durations and play melodies is through your own knowledge of the song. If you know the melody and the durations that come with it by heart, you will be able to follow the rhythm and give proper durations. This can be slightly more complicated for melodies because all notes located within a measure tend to have varying durations. These varying durations have a set purpose and created a melody in its proper form. Once you know of the durations, you can tell just when to change notes for generating proper melody. There are melodies you know by heart, and you can practice durations on these melodies to perfect your style.

Play from Notated Tablature

Tablature can also have notated numbers. These notations are meant to show the durations between melodies. A notated tablature can give you a sense of direction to follow while playing the music on the ukulele.

You can always learn how to interpret note durations when you become a more accomplished uke player. For now, you must understand the importance of these durations, and what you need to do for further results..

Chapter Fifteen

Understanding the Anatomy of Sheet Music for the Ukulele

Music, which has been written to be played on the ukulele, can be visible in one of the following three formats:

- Song sheets, which include both chords and lyrics and is perfectly suited for performing groups;
- Standard musical notation within a lead sheet, which is easy to be played by anyone with a basic understanding of music;
- In the form of tablature, which can be used instead of musical notation.

The musical notes for playing the ukulele are further discussed below:

Standard Music Notation within the Treble Clef

In addition to the notes of the chords and melodies, the treble clef is also perfect for showing the song key and time signature. All musicians who have played a standard musical notation before would know everything there is to know about it. Standard musical notation includes everything that you need or require for playing a song. Chords are represented through letter symbols in the standard musical notation and are placed for the benefit of the uke player. They are adequately placed for players who just want to play the chords.

This is the reason why we have a capital F written over all the notes to be played for the chord F and an adequate Am written all over the notes which are played for the A minor chord. You don't need to have an in-depth knowledge of chords and notes to be able to play the ukulele. What you do need to know is just how you should finger the A minor chord and the F chord and strum properly to the rhythm of the music. This information is enough to get you started.

Song Sheets: Chords and Words Only

Song sheets are more popular with beginner level players because they show information in a form that is easier for them to interpret. Song sheets include just the chord symbols and lyrics in a form, which is easy for the newbie to understand. These sheets emit all tablature and treble clefs, as they can be a bit hard for beginners to understand and comprehend.

Anyone familiar with song sheets will know just how much information is presented in one. There are just chords and words. You can easily tell when you are required to play a chord or to skip an uncommon chord. The information is predictable and does not require additional interpretation.

Tablature Showing Melodies and Chords

If you do not know how to read music, and do not understand how to manually finger chords, then a tablature will have all the information you need. Sometimes a tablature is all you have for playing the ukulele, as you have to work around the information given to generate soulful bits of music for the ears. Whenever you see notes that are stacked in a tablature, you have to strum all four of the strings on your uke. The tablature is easy to understand and play.

There are multiple sheets for referencing to when playing music on the ukulele. All of these sheets are meant to make your work easier as a musician. Through these sheets, you can make playing the ukulele easier for yourself, without having to look up obscure chords or take up challenging interpretations.

Chapter Sixteen

Songs to Play on the Ukulele

By now, you know how to play the ukulele at a basic level and how to manage the chords and the notes. Playing the ukulele is no mean feat, which is why you have got all the reasons to be proud of yourself.

The ukulele is one of those rare musical instruments which is capable of lighting up the mood within any place. The instrument is easy to play and makes for some good entertainment and fun time with your friends. It just takes a couple of chords to get everyone smiling when you have a ukulele in your hands and some basic info on how to manage the instrument. Improving your skillset on the ukulele might take some time, but it doesn't really have to be boring at any cost. Through the course of this book, you might have found out just how interesting and exciting the entire prospect of playing the ukulele can be. You get to enjoy the new stuff and can play to your full potential wherever and whenever you want.

The entire stage of learning how to play the ukulele can be fun as well, as you find out interesting and new ways of handling the instrument in the best manner possible. The experience is fun and will give you plenty of things to learn and develop.

In this chapter, we are going to delve into the world of uke magic and will talk about some of the best songs that you can play on your prized instrument. These songs will be challenging to master for all beginners when they are just starting out their journey, but let us tell you that they can be gratifying, as you rope in praise and honor from everyone around you.

We take this as an excuse to include some of the classics as well, which will help you in amusing your friends and family in an even better manner. Well, classics can be a bit hard to play when you're doing them the first time, but let us tell you, the gratification is just worth it.

Each one of the songs that we have mentioned in this list has made its way to the top because of a reason. All of these songs make playing the ukulele a lot simpler and give you the kind of musical brilliance you are looking for. All of these songs sound amazing on the ukulele, which is why you don't have to worry about them losing their basic essence when you strum on them.

Warm Up and Prep

Before we start with the list, it is best for you as a beginner to take a deep breath and do some warm-up steps. Taking up these big songs can be a challenge, which is why you have to be ready for what is coming your way. Some very amazing players of the ukulele have messed up a simple song routine because they weren't mentally prepared to start playing. So, before we get to the music, you have to sit down and reflect on whether you are mentally prepared to be playing this music. If you think you are mentally prepared for the challenge, there is nothing that should be stopping you.

You can plan to practice singing as well alongside the songs, which will add further purpose to your performance. Singing alongside the performance will give you the kind of gratification you want and will surely get your audience all riled up. Do a vocal warm-up routine before you head to the stage and start your routine to amuse your viewers.

If you're not sure over how to go about tuning your vocal cords, you can go through plenty of guide videos available on the internet. These videos have plenty of helpful info and can help you decide the best way forward for tuning your vocal cords for the performance that is to come. You do not want to mess your performance up because your vocals weren't tuned properly. It is important that you also practice singing for lengthy sessions so that you know you are fully prepared for what is to come. Do not push yourself when it comes to singing. You do not want to be overwhelming your vocal cords, as doing so can lead to multiple repercussions.

With all of this said and done, it is time we jumped into some of the best songs to play on your ukulele. These songs will keep you hooked and will surely give you the acclaim you deserve.

TIP: Learn to play (and sing!) songs. Don't just fiddle around with it. The purpose of music is to play songs, not to just make sound.

Somewhere over the Rainbow/What a Wonderful World by Israel Kamakawiwo'ole

There is no better way to start practicing the ukulele than this wonderful masterpiece by the legend Israel Kamakawiwo'ole. We believe you can pull this off with your ukulele because it isn't really that challenging. This song is an amalgam of two different classics, which is why you need to be careful with how you pull the strings together. You won't just be paying homage to one classic, but will be doing so to two in one go.

If we look at it, the individual pieces weren't so great for playing together on a ukulele. But the way Israel fused the whole song goes a long way into making this the perfect piece to play on your newly learned ukulele. The world of Harold Arlen and Bob Thiele has been fused for you, and all you need to do is step up and take the challenge. Mix the personas of both these stars and create magic with your ukulele.

If we look at the basics, mastering this song on the uke can take a lot of time. Obviously, certain notes will be harder for you to pull, but believe us when we say that this brilliant amalgam will end up teaching you just what you need to know about the chords and patterns of strumming. The music is easier to manage and is just a delight to listen to.

Somewhere over the Rainbow/What a Wonderful World by Israel Kamakawiwo'ole might not be the easiest song for you to learn on your ukulele, but it is one that will tell you a lot about how the uke is played, and what you can do to further your information. Since we know you are just starting out, the information mentioned in this book will help you do that. We encourage you to ace this song and try some of the other songs that Israel has done, he is a true genius on the ukulele, and if you can replicate his success, you'd be doing a lot of things right.

Jason Mraz – I'm Yours

I'm yours by Jason Mraz is a more contemporary addition to this list. In fact, if you are one for classics and classical, traditional music, you might not have heard this one. Nothing beats the melody and soothing music that Jason Mraz has been able to produce in this song. This is one of the few awesome songs to have come out in the last few years, and you can try it out on your ukulele.

The good thing about this song is that Mraz kept things fairly simple with the music. He didn't over-experiment, which is why he ended up getting the best results. The song has been molded to match the mainstream standards of today's audiences, but most of it the same as it was back in the day.

The chord progression for this soulful bit of music is just what excites us the most. The chord progressions are found to be closer to modern pop music in the spectrum of music, which is why most ukulele players will be able to master it without much ado. You can sing this song along with playing the ukulele because the lyrics are just as catchy and exciting as the music that comes out of your ukulele.

We believe this song is an amazing choice for every little kid looking to sing along while playing the music. This song gives you a good option to perfect your vocals while working on a great melody. The melody for this song will steer your vocals forward as well and will help you improve your overall performance as a whole.

Once you start playing 'I'm Yours' by Jason Mraz, you will notice that the strumming pattern used here is fairly simple. We have talked in detail about strumming methods and techniques, and you ought to know all about them by now. The simple strumming techniques used within this song give you a chance to innovate and bring up a new technique that can come in handy. The new technique doesn't necessarily have to be extremely complex, but you can change the strumming pattern, as there is significant room for improvisation. The song teaches you a lot of interesting things that you can later implement within your own music.

Can't Help Falling In Love by Elvis Presley

Elvis Presley was a genius, and he created some of the best songs you will hear. Can't Help Falling In Love is a classic by Elvis Presley and is one of the best songs that he has played. The song has a soulful melody to it and can be played on the ukulele, as it has a consistent tone that won't challenge you.

The beauty of this song lies in just how much room for innovation and improvisation you have here. You can innovate while playing the song and can try some out of the box tricks that aren't on the sheet. There are multiple ways for you to play this song, and we believe that every method has its own charm. The song, if perfected, will create a gentle melody on the ukulele and will get you all the praise and acclaim that you are looking for.

The chord progression within this song is basic, and there are no complexities as such. You can follow the basic chord progression, which is inherently part of this song, or you can make things a bit spicier by adding subtle details within the mix. The fact remains that you have a lot to learn from the music here.

Since most beginners are confused about where to start from, we might have some helpful tips for you. You can start off with an easy pattern for strumming, before moving over to the chords mentioned. As soon as you get the hang of how the chords progress, you can change your strumming pattern while maintaining the rhythm and making sure that the new strumming pattern is in line with the original tone of the song. We believe that singing along to this song isn't really a bad idea, as it would give you a decent learning curve. There is plenty to learn here, which is why you can walk away with a lot more knowledge than what you first bargained for. The song has good and strong vocals, which will surely enhance your own performance as well.

Just like all of the songs that we have tried to list here, Can't Help Falling in Love is one of those everyday tunes, which will never fall out of favor with the masses. The tune will never grow old, and you can play it whenever you are outside on a campfire with your friends. This is one for the ages.

Trouble by Never Shout Never

The songs we have listed so far are for beginners to get their feet wet on the ukulele. Once you have learned how to play them, you can jump on to Trouble by Never Shout Never. This is one of the more complex songs to sing and play on the ukulele, which is why this will act like the progression you need in your journey towards glory. This song is a bit different than others because it isn't just considered challenging because of the tune or uke notes, but because of something else.

To be honest, the music in this song is just as simple as it gets. The chords and strumming patterns are easy to keep a hold of, and you can easily follow them without a worry in the world. The value this song holds as a learning tool comes from someplace else, and not just the complexity of the strumming patterns.

No kidding, if there was a song that can challenge you when it comes to playing it and singing together, then it is this one. Trouble by Never Shout Never is one of the hardest songs to sing while playing it on the ukulele as well. By complex, we're talking non-congruent verses, extreme changes in the tempo, rhythm that goes against the verses, and a lot more.

However, being able to perform this song flawlessly will be one of the most gratifying feelings ever and will act as a feather in your cap. You need to start playing this song slow so that you can take it to the next level without any issues whatsoever.

The intro is classy and requires you to play a single chord four times. This continuous repetition develops as a strumming pattern later during the song. You will obviously find challenges when trying to sing and play this song together. The best way to tackle these challenges is to learn how to play this song first on the ukulele. Once you have perfected your playing pattern, you can then work on the singing to lend your vocals. This will allow you to go at your own pace and make some necessary modifications to the rhythm.

Let us warn you that learning how to play this song will take some time. The entire process will drain the life out of you, and you might even think about trying something other than playing the ukulele, but it is worth it. The lyrics will also force you to broaden the limits of your singing capabilities at the time, but let us tell you that every bit of it would be worth it. From the progression and development, you witness as a uke player, to the enhancements in your vocal skills, every bit of it would be worth it.

Riptide by Vance Joy

Sung by Vance Joy, Riptide is one of the most amazing songs for you to play on the ukulele. However, you need to be a follower of contemporary and more modern music, if you really want to enjoy this song. The song has a simple chord progression and is pretty simple for beginner level uke players to play on their equipment. There is nothing too complex about this song, but there are interesting phases where you might be challenged by the sudden twists and turns in the music. The rhythm goes up and down and requires expert-level skills.

The strumming pattern used within this song resembles the strumming pattern that was common in the class guitar aesthetics of traditional Spanish songs. The strumming pattern for traditional Spanish songs would require the player to jump from one chord to another without taking any undue breaks. The strumming will sound amazing on the ukulele, but the strumming pattern will challenge your abilities and would require you to go from one chord to another without taking a break.

You will have to be quick with your strumming pattern here, as you don't have a lot of time between songs here. Quickly jumping from one chord to another is what will define success for you as someone playing the fretboard here.

Whether the quick chord progression is a problem for you will depend on the current skill set you boast of. The quick progression can turn out to be a problem for you if you are just starting to learn how to play the ukulele. A beginner will take around a couple of weeks to play the whole song within its original form.

Things can, however, get a bit tricky if you are looking to sing this song as well. Vance Joy is an amazing singer, and he has shown his vocal range in full glory within this song. If you don't have full control over your vocals yet, you won't be able to deliver on some of the notes like he has been able to. However, if you have control over your chords, you will be able to do an amazing job with this song.

La Vie En Rose by Edith Piaf

La Vie En Rose by Edith Piaf is one of those amazing and iconic songs, which has been played or interpreted on almost all different kinds of popular instruments. La Vie En Rose is one of the best ballads ever performed and is also one of the best sons for beginner-level ukulele players to try.

The best part about this song is that you can easily adapt it according to your own playing and singing style. You don't have to follow the style chosen by the singer to the tee and can make your own adjustments to it. If you are impressed by the legendary Edith and want to do it in her way, then you will have to send your voice into overdrive and sing in a manner that would be in line with what Edith did here.

The standard uke strumming pattern works just fine here. There is room for improvisation, but considering your current level of expertise, we would want you to go with the flow, as improvisations can be risky here. You can arpeggiate the chords if you feel like adding an improvised touch to the tone or want to speed things up. The improvisation rests entirely on your shoulders.

Talking about rarity, this is one of the few songs that will sound sad and dramatic even on a ukulele. You can play the song really slow to break down the chords into notes. The song will give you a blue tone and will surely get those tears rolling. This is one of the few songs that can make a performer cry.

Hallelujah by Leonard Cohen

Continuing on the list of sad ballads that make amazing ukulele songs, Hallelujah by the late Leonard Cohen comes to mind. We might have lost Leonard Cohen very recently, but his work is still there for people to enjoy and recreate. Anyone who has listened to the song would know of the energy that comes from it. Interestingly, playing the song on a ukulele takes none of the energy away from it, and instead adds a lot more of exuberance and passion.

There are plenty of performers who have played Hallelujah on the ukulele and have been able to ace the routine. If you can match the melody of the ukulele with some amazing vocals, you'd be doing the late soul of Leonard Cohen, a great service.

This song is a perfect learning curve to boost your ukulele skills as well. This can be said because the song creates an extremely special vibe, which you surely cannot create with any other instrument. The rhythm and accentuating chords help broaden your skillset and give you a lot more to learn and practice. The song might start slowly, but it soon picks up the pace and becomes as intense as you would want it to be. It does take some practice to ace the song, as you will at first be all over the place trying to perfect the rhythm.

Hey, Soul Sister by Train

Unlike the previous couple of songs, there is nothing sad about Hey, Soul Sister by Train. The song is melodious and perfectly suited for your ukulele. The strumming pattern is as basic as they come, and you don't need any special skills to master. This song is a great mood lifter for whoever is listening or playing it. You can lift your mood as a player, because you don't need any new skills to play this song, and because you can easily manage the strumming pattern. Are there times when you feel low and down as a uke player? Well, this is the song to play at that time.

The chords for this song are easy, and the lyrics have a high pitched tonality. Vocals can be hard, because Hey, Soul Sister does not sound the same without these high vocals and tonality. This might put off a few people from playing this song, but once you complement your lyrics with the ease of playing the notes for this song, you get a gratifying mix. Singing this song can help push your voice across new limits and heights.

Blank Space by Taylor Swift

Not many would expect this song to be a popular entry within the ukulele crowd, but it is what it is. This amazing song by Taylor Swift is catchy to listen to and has simple chord progression. Playing this song on the ukulele is fairly easy and does not require endless maneuvering. You can easily find your way around the challenging vocals since the ukulele chords are fairly easy.

Blank Space is slowly and gradually becoming one of the most popular ukulele songs, much to the craze of the younger crowds towards Taylor Swift. The happy tune can easily be played, which we believe is one reason why.

Another good part about this song is that you can choose to go happy with it or can take the blue route out. Your singing can determine just how you go about this whole song. The singing pattern does not have to be consistent and by the sheets. You can play around a bit with the strumming pattern as well, as you can infuse a variety of emotions within this song. Blank Space is, in fact, a Blank Canvass, waiting for you to be filled or played on your ukulele in a manner you want.

Hello by Adele

All contemporary followers of music will recall Hello by Adele. The song lit the world up and broke the internet in no time. Knowing just how much success the song had roped in within a short time, it was no surprise seeing it makes its way into the world of ukuleles and other instruments.

It was only when people started playing the song on the ukulele, did they realize just how much sense it made. The melody is simple and relatively easy to learn. You don't have to learn a lot of new things, as the strumming is fairly easy to manage. The hard part here is that you will have to decide between playing this song a bit faster and turning it into a sad ballad. Regardless of which path you choose, you have to make sure that you accentuate the strumming with some powerful vocals. Playing the song faster can give a more pop-like feel to it, which would make even Adele proud.

Hello, by Adele, sounds great, regardless of how you plan to play it. The song has powerful melodies and is relatively easy to play on the ukulele.

Creep by Radiohead

This is one song that has been perfectly made to be played on the ukulele. You might think of this as crazy, but only once you play the song on your ukulele, will you realize just how perfectly it has been toned for a ukulele. The song is a bit tricky to play with all the chord progression, but it has an undeniable emotional attachment and drive, which will blow your mind off.

Creep can be played in a lot of different ways, with all of the methods giving you the perfect results you might be looking for. The original vocals might be hard and melancholic, but they follow the pattern, so you don't have to innovate much.

You can innovate with the song by raising the tonality a bit. This will add a lot of brightness to the piece, and will still allow it to sound amazing. We think Creep by Radiohead is surely one of the best songs to be played on the Ukulele. If you want to take the music for this song onto a whole other level, you can try arpeggiating it into smaller chords. This will help the song sound even better and will make a world of difference.

The A-Team by Ed Sheeran

Ed Sheeran is another star very famous with the younger generation, which is exactly why younger fans have played many of his songs on the ukulele. His climb to fame has been awesome as he is an amazing producer and lyricist as well.

The A-Team by Ed Sheeran is one of the more melodious songs to play on the ukulele in general. The song has a lot more chords than other songs, but many of these chords are just barre chords. The good part about this song is that you have the luxury to make it as complex and as simple as you want. There is plenty of room for innovation and improvement. You can add your own touch to the music and can feel good about it.

Many uke players want to spice things up by adding touches here and there for better results. This is the kind of song you would want to play if you are that kind of player. You can also use the standard strumming pattern for ukes if you don't want to be creative.

All of Me by John Legend

The final tune we have here is one of the most challenging songs to ace on the ukulele. The song is a definite hit with the masses, and you might have heard it quite a few times as well. All of Me by John Legend is the love anthem of the youth today, and you might have come across it at some stage in time.

What you can do to make this song amazing on the uke while retaining the power John Legend lent to his version is to arpeggiate the verses and chords appropriately. Chord progression is not simple and requires a lot of practice.

The best part is when you jump from the arpeggiated version to the standard ukulele strumming patterns. This will deliver a punch of energy to the song and will push it onto a whole new level.

Vocals aren't hard, but only if you know how to hit the chords right. The chorus has several high notes, which you can play in a manner that you deem best. Once you have comfortably settled into the world of John Legend and his love anthem, you will see friends begging you to play it for you.

In this chapter, we have listed some of the best songs to play on the ukulele. Many of these are classics and have a class of their own. The modern pieces we have mentioned as well are fairly popular with the masses and make the songs even better to listen to. The whole idea behind this list is to get you into practicing and gradually increasing your skillset. We've introduced you to tunes that require marginal levels of strumming and singing. These songs will make you feel good about the lessons you have acquired within this book and will help you in boosting your skillset even further.

TIP: UkuTabs.com is great place to learn songs for the uke

Conclusion

Your journey as a ukulele player does not end with this book. Instead, it is just beginning. This is where you start your journey and build upon what you have learned in order to become a professional. By now, you know enough to play some basic strings and follow some simple strumming patterns on the ukulele, and this is where the fun begins! Now it's time to practice. A lot! As you continue to practice, grow, and develop as a musician, the world will continue to open its musical doors to you. The sky is the limit!

References

https://consordini.com/ukulele-explained-all-you-need-to-know/

https://www.ukulelemag.com/stories/your-first-ukulele-lesson-a-beginners-guide-to-playing-ukulele

https://coustii.com/ukulele-chords-beginners/

https://ukuguides.com/beginner/10-ukulele-tips-for-beginners/

https://acousticbridge.com/types-of-ukuleles/

https://consordini.com/best-ukulele-songs/

www.ingramcontent.com/pod-product-compliance
Lightning Source LLC
Chambersburg PA
CBHW071520080526
44588CB00011B/1496